the X diet cookbook

TABITHA HUME

Published by Zebra Press
(an imprint of Struik New Holland Publishing (Pty) Ltd)
PO Box 1144, Cape Town 8000
Tel: +27 21 462 4360
Fax: +27 21 462 4379

First edition published in 1999

10 9 8 7 6 5 4

Published work © Zebra Press 1999
Text © Tabitha Hume 1999
Photographs © John Peacock 1999

All rights reserved. No part of this publication may be reproduced, stored in a retrieval system or transmitted, in any form or by any means, electronic, mechanical, photocopying, recording or otherwise, without the prior written permission of the copyright owners.

Managing editor   Marika Truter
Copy editors   Vicky Hanson & Jane-Anne Hobbs
Cover designer   Lindy Truswell
Book designer   Lindy Truswell
Photographer   John Peacock

Reproduction by Remata Bureau & Printers, Midrand
Printed and bound by NBD, Drukkery Street, Goodwood 7460, Western Cape

ISBN 1-86872-080-2

Thank you to Loads of Linen, Emmarentia, for generously providing crockery and cutlery.

contents

Foreword	iv
Acknowledgements	v
Introduction	vi
Basics of The X Diet	viii
Fat-Free Cooking	xi
Starters	1
Soups	7
Salads	17
Vegetables	25
Family Favourites	39
Fish & Seafood	49
Chicken	63
Desserts	75
Baking	83
Sauces	89
Recipe Index	92

a husband's view

The story of how I met Tabitha is directly related to food. I was a busy young bachelor working at a large bank; dieting and good eating habits were at the bottom of my list of priorities. A colleague and friend, who had been following Tabitha's diet and whose middle-aged physique had turned into that of a young man, recommended a visit to Tabitha. I phoned, made an appointment, and then forgot about the whole thing. The day I was due to see her, I unfortunately had to cancel, and also didn't reschedule the appointment.

We later met, by pure chance, while holidaying in the Eastern Cape. There was an immediate attraction. What also struck me at the time was that here was a girl with a voracious appetite (who could consume as much food as I could, and with much more enthusiasm than I had ever seen in a woman) yet whose figure was not the least of the things that attracted me to her.

When we returned to Johannesburg, we met for coffee, dated for three weeks, got engaged and married at the end of 1998. I have now eaten Tabitha's fat-free food for the last year and a half, and so feel well qualified to speak on the subject.

When we measured my metabolism we found that I did not process food as quickly as I should. We decided I should give her diet a go. What Tabitha told me seemed very exciting:
1. Beer does not make you fat (at the time I drank a lot of beer).
2. Sugar does not make you fat (I have always had at least two teaspoons in coffee and tea, and drink about 20 cups a day).
3. McDonald's hamburgers are basically good, and are not the root of all dietary evils.
4. Pizzas are a food group all on their own.

This all seemed very heartening, since I lived on pizza, McDonald's and beer (in that order), and did not relish the thought of giving any of them up.

For the next two weeks I was weaned off all fat. I learnt how to eat a phenomenal amount but did not touch anything with fat in it. I ate huge bowls of cereal and vast quantities of fruit for breakfast, got the canteen to make me toasted chicken sandwiches without butter or mayonnaise for snacks, and ate enough food at dinner to feed my entire division at the bank. I was forbidden from eating my favourite pizza (spicy chicken with bacon, feta and extra mozzarella) and even had to give up McDonald's! I wondered where the exciting part came in, but was so in love with my fiancée that I did as I was told.

By the end of the two weeks, my metabolism had increased by about 33% and I had more energy than I knew what to do with. Then, the results: my metabolism was now sufficiently equipped to handle my beloved pizzas and hamburgers! We started going to restaurants again, and I dug into my old menu with the enthusiasm I last felt on my first pass from basic training.

Tabitha taught me how to choose 'basically fat-free' items from restaurant menus, and introduced me to a world where fat-free eating is a great, rewarding and delicious experience. Whenever people who know Tabitha meet me, the first question they ask is, 'Do you also have to eat this way?' To them, fat free means boiled fish and steamed vegetables. My reply is well practised: 'I eat better than any man I know, my wife's food is the best I have ever been lucky enough to try, I have pizzas at least twice a week, and regularly enjoy a quarter-pounder with cheese.'

I have managed to start wearing clothes that I discarded long ago, and have more energy at work than any of my colleagues. One of my business partners continually expresses dismay at the fact that I always eat more fat than I should. He doesn't understand the metabolism change that has freed me to make my own rules. I may have more fat in a single meal than all my colleagues put together but, over a week, consume less fat than they do in three months.

Although I may lack objectivity, I am well qualified to highly recommend the recipes in this book. Whether you are looking for a way of adding creativity to your fat-free lifestyle, or are simply looking for delicious meals that you can cook easily (even I can cook some of these recipes), I think this is the book for you. Read, try and enjoy!

David Edwards
Johannesburg
September 1999

acknowledgements

I would like to thank several people for their hard work in putting together this wonderful book:

Our patients and their families - without your generous contribution to the development of these recipes, this book would not have happened.
Lena Kgoro, our invaluable kitchen executive - your contribution to many of the delicious recipes we indulge in has been invaluable.
Toni and *David Hume*, my parents - your presence and creative energy has been my anchor.
Dorothy Tristao, Marie-Therese Ringel, Henriette Stoddard, Nicole Sacks, Annabel Mostert, Tamaryn Holzinger and *Emma Seymour* - The X Clinic team, who made all the difference.

Zebra Press, and especially my publisher, *Marika Truter* - you had the vision to see the difference between just another slimming recipe book and this gorgeous creation, and the creative energy to make it happen.

Jane-Anne Hobbs and *Vicky Hanson*, two wonderful editors - you taught us how to turn our passion for food into something clear enough to read, understand, and easily get stuck into! Jane-Anne, congratulations on your new little baby girl! We don't know how you managed to work right up to the last hour!
John Peacock - your incredible photographs have shown all X Dieters how beautiful our delicious fat-free food can look.
Lynn Melrose - your creative styling has enhanced the recipes to something beautiful and sensuous.
Lindy Truswell - your innovate design captured the feel of the book perfectly.

David Edwards, my husband - your sampling of all the recipes and your offerings of blunt criticism ensured that these dishes really are good enough for any South African man to indulge in.

introduction

This is a collection of delicious fat-free recipes developed in response to numerous requests from my patients during my years as a dietician.

I developed the X Diet, a fat-free eating plan, as a therapy for people suffering from the major lifestyle diseases that are now understood by medical science to be symptoms of a broader 'umbrella' disorder, namely Metabolic Syndrome, or Syndrome X. These symptoms include fat gain and obesity, cholesterol problems, high blood pressure, heart disease, adult-onset diabetes, kidney disease and perhaps even polycystic ovaria syndrome. In a nutshell, the idea behind the X Diet is to increase the amount of carbohydrates we eat, whilst lowering blood sugar levels and insulin, and to eliminate as much fat from the diet as possible.

In the past, lowering blood sugar levels meant eating less. This led to many metabolic problems, as well as profound psychological ones. So we tried to cut out fats, like butter, meat fats and cheese, for instance. The problems persisted, and it is now that we realise that simply cutting out visible fats isn't enough. Because our modern lifestyle means sedentary habits and remote-control existences, we need to reduce fats even more than this, and this means cutting out the hidden fats in foods. This way, we can eat a diet with fat levels as low as 3% of total calories.

As the X Diet evolved, a major problem presented itself: how was I to convince my patients to eliminate the killer fats from their diets and at the same time persuade them that the foods they would eat instead were so scrumptious and satisfying that they would never feel the slightest inclination to 'cheat'? 'Do you mean no oil at all, not even olive oil?' they would say. 'Not even a scraping of butter? I can't live like that!'

Who could blame these patients for feeling unenthusiastic? When you look at the sort of food that is offered up by popular calorie-cutting diets and dieting clubs, it's no wonder that people never stick to diets for long, and that they end up gaining more fat than they had in the first place. For too long we, the dieting public, have been led to believe that eating healthily is synonymous with eating tasteless, dry, boring and bland food – food that bears no resemblance to the sort of food we actually feel like eating. The people who seem to formulate these extra low fat recipes or cholesterol cookbooks tend to be those who have learnt to deny themselves of the genuinely indulgent properties of food. They claim that a diet laden with steamed vegetables and steamed rice and with few flavourings really should be enjoyed as much as a dreamy, creamy lasagne!

I think it is vital to acknowledge how important a role food plays in our happiness and well-being. We celebrate special occasions with food and we socialise over food. We eat food to comfort ourselves, to reward ourselves and to satisfy our most profound physiological and emotional needs. How can we possibly be expected to deny ourselves such an enormous and wonderful part of our existence?

The answer, I realised, was to prove to my patients that, with a little imagination and a few easy techniques, it is possible to create the most succulent and flavourful of meals – without reaching for the bottle of oil.

When taking down patients' reports of what they have been eating since being on the X Diet, there is a preponderance of pasta with tomato and onion sauce, grilled chicken breasts with lemon and herbs, and my personal 'favourite', fish baked in foil with onion, tomato and herbs.

If the patient had never been on a diet, he/she would probably never have chosen these dishes in the first place. They are good to eat, but place each of these next to a chicken schnitzel with cheese sauce, or a rich bobotie, and few people would have difficulty in choosing. Even when we ask patients to tell us what they would really love to have for supper, they still suggest things such as salads, the formidable tomato pasta or grilled chicken breast!

Where has the passion for multiple flavours gone? Have we become so indoctrinated by 'health' that we have completely forgotten what our taste buds really want? People seem to make enjoyment of exciting food synonymous with guilt: if this food really turns me on, then it will really turn to fat!

It is for this reason that we have insisted on three fairly harsh 'sentences':

1. Tomato pasta, grilled chicken breast fillets and baked fish in lemon and herbs are actually forbidden amongst our patients. Firstly, because it blatantly shows that the patient is still wrapped up in the 'diet mentality', and secondly because their families will not enjoy this food (Those most honest about enjoying food are men and children!) The patient will therefore resort to eating separately from the family, because she/he feels guilty about subjecting them to her/his 'punishment' for being overweight. This is the first step to the self-admonishment that leads to psychological trauma and low self-esteem, as well as problems with sticking to a diet.

2. The patient must eat with the whole family, as this will help get rid of all dieting mentalities, and encourage her/him to produce good food, which she/he will inadvertently want to continue eating for a much longer time, as there will be no feelings of deprivation.

3. The patient must replace a conventional dieting method with a new one. Instead of thinking, 'What is there left that I can have, and how can I put it together creatively?', she/he must now practice thinking, 'What is it that I would really love to have if I wasn't eating healthily, and how do I make it fat free?'

In this way, the patient will not think of pasta mixed with tomato and onion sauce but will learn to be honest, and admit that a creamy lasagne would actually be more appealing. If you read on, you may be astonished that you are able to indulge completely in all your favourites, without wanting anything else at all – and they are fat free!! It is with these principles in mind that I set about developing a range of tempting recipes specifically designed to satisfy the sorts of cravings that frequently plague anyone placed on a strict eating regime. I constantly demanded from my patients that they voice their 'complaints' about my eating plan. 'What is it that you are craving?' I would ask. 'What do you really miss?'. 'If you think of your favourite meal, without the worry of health, what would that 'naughty' meal be?'

'Bangers and mash with gravy,' one patient would say, and I would rise to the challenge, heading directly to the kitchen after work to figure out a way of mimicking a meal that usually swims in fat. 'Pasta with creamy Alfredo sauce,' another person would wail, and very soon I would produce a substitute that tasted just as good but contained a microscopic amount of fat.

Very soon my patients and friends started contributing recipes of their own, and a small collection of dog-eared, chutney-smeared pieces of paper started to grow into a recipe book.

I tested the recipes on friends and family without letting on that what they were eating was fat free, paying particular attention to those friends whom I know prided themselves on their fussy palates. At many a dinner party in those early months my friends would demolish a platter of pasta or chicken, saying, 'It's delicious! Tell me, what did you put in this?' Never once did they guess that all these meals were made without fat.

For three years now I have personally followed a fat-free eating regime, and I have never felt healthier, happier or more energetic. I certainly never feel deprived – and believe me, I am as passionate about good food as it is possible to be.

Fat-free eating does not mean saying good-bye to the foods you love, or waving a fond farewell to pancakes, apple muffins or creamy chicken à la king. Read on, and you will see that what it does mean is eating like a king, enjoying your meals and indulging in the food you love without experiencing the slightest guilt. In fact, when a patient is told that they should try and eat like this for ever, and their expressions drop, I know that I am about to enlighten yet another diet victim with indulgence they never thought possible! Believe me, it is a joy showing people that this way of eating is actually nicer than the way they were eating before. If a patient leaves our practice without excessive salivation, then we have failed.

Eat, drink and be merry!

Tabitha Hume
Johannesburg
September 1999

the basics of the X diet

Here is a 21-step summary of the basics of the X Diet, as outlined in my book *The X Diet*. You might want to photocopy this chapter and stick it on your fridge or grocery cupboard for quick and easy reference.

Important note: Some of the guidelines, such as the advice about eating vast quantities of carbohydrates, may seem at best confusing and at worst like heresy, particularly if you are a seasoned dieter or a fan of calorie-cutting diets. If this is the case, I urge you to read *The X Diet* from cover to cover, if you have not already done so. In order to gain the full benefit of the X Diet, it's vital that you thoroughly understand the principles involved.

1. CUT OUT ALL FATS

All plant fats and all animal fats should be eliminated from your diet. These include:

x Olive oil, sunflower oil, other plant oils, salad dressings, mayonnaise, salad creams and Spray 'n Cook
x Avocados, coconut, coconut cream and palm kernel oil
x Nuts and seeds of all kinds
x Butter, margarine, cream, sour cream, full-cream and low-fat milk, full-cream and low-fat yoghurt, coffee creamers and cheese. Only fat-free dairy products are permitted
x Egg yolks (whites are permitted)
x All red meats and organ meats. These include beef, pork, lamb, mutton, liver, kidneys, tripe, and processed meats such as sausages, spreads and pâtés. (Even commercially available vegetarian sausages are forbidden.)
x Fatty fish, including sardines, pilchards, salmon, mackerel, herrings and anchovies
x Products containing hidden fats, such as crisps, pastries, biscuits, rusks, chocolate, sauces and so on

2. COOK FAT FREE

This means a lot more than just not using oils or butter! It also means watching out for hidden fats in pre-made sauces and other convenience products. All sauces, such as white sauce, should be made without fat. If you need to sautée food, do so using the 'dry-fry' method (*see page xi*). This method should be learnt before starting anything, because not using it dramatically cuts down on flavour. Use only non-stick pans for baking. Recipes can be helpful, but remember that many recipes that claim to be 'low fat' or even 'fat free' contain small amounts of oil or butter. Remember, no fat at all!

3. READ THE LABELS

Do not be conned by misleading words and icons on packaging, such as 'diet', 'lite', 'low-fat' and 'slimmer's'. Check the fat content of every product you buy *(see below)*. If the fat content is not listed on the label, carefully check the list of ingredients for hidden fats.

4. REMEMBER THE 'GOLDEN THREE-GRAM RULE'

Buy only those foods that contain less than 3 g of fat per 100 g of product. For the purposes of the X Diet, these are considered fat free and may be eaten in unlimited quantities. Please don't be caught by percentages: 2% fat does not mean 2 g of fat per 100 g! (What it does mean is too complex to explain in detail here.) Also, make sure that foods contain less than 3 g of fat per 100 g and not per 10 g serving, in which case the food would contain a lot more fat than first appears!

5. EAT AS MUCH NON-FATTY FISH AS YOU LIKE

Non-fatty fish such as hake, kingklip, kabeljou, sole and tuna tinned in brine may be eaten freely.

6. EAT AS MUCH SHELLFISH AS YOU LIKE

Prawns, shrimps, crayfish, mussels, oysters and calamari are freely allowed. If you are concerned about your cholesterol levels, we have discovered that animal fats and total fats in the diet are responsible for elevated cholesterol levels, not dietary cholesterol. Be careful, however, in the way you cook them.

7. EAT BREAST FILLET OF CHICKEN

You may eat limited quantities of skinned, deboned chicken breasts (about three to six a week). The skin, fat and fatty flesh of chicken are not permitted on the X Diet.

8 EAT AS MANY 'POLISH' FOODS AS YOU CAN

'Polish' foods include all fruits, salads and vegetables (with the exception of avocados, olives, coconuts, nuts and seeds) and all fat-free dairy products. Let me stress here that you should eat as many 'polish' foods as you can, not as many as you want! At the very least, you must eat three to four fruits a day, but the more the better.

9. EAT THE 'SPECIAL SEVEN' VEGETABLES EVERY DAY

Eat at least a cup a day of vegetables that are rich in beta-carotene – the rich orange, the dark green and leafy, and the deep purple veggies. The 'special seven' are butternut, pumpkin, spinach, broccoli, carrots, beetroot and red cabbage. These can be eaten raw or lightly cooked, fresh or frozen.

10. EAT PLENTY OF CARBOHYDRATES

Ensure that you eat enough carbohydrates for your metabolic rate. For most people, this usually entails doubling (or even tripling!) their daily carbohydrate intake. The exact quantity depends, however, on your individual needs and on any health problems you may have.

11. EAT HIGH-GI CARBOHYDRATES TO BUILD MUSCLE AND SPEED METABOLISM

High-GI foods are those with a high glycaemic index: that is, they quickly dissolve into their component sugars. If your aim is to build muscle bulk and to speed your metabolism, eat plenty of high-GI carbohydrates, such as bread, potatoes, sugar, honey and cereals.

12. EAT LOW-GI FOODS TO BURN FAT

If your main aim is to burn fat, cut down on high-GI carbohydrates, and eat plenty of low-GI carbohydrates. These are foods with a low glycaemic index, namely those that dissolve slowly in the gut, releasing sugar into the bloodstream gradually. They include beans, sweetcorn, white rice, pasta, lentils, barley, soya beans, soya mince, peas, fructose and oats. If you would like to speed up your metabolism at the same time, include some high-GI foods *(see above)* in your diet.

13. DRINK PLENTY OF WATER

You must drink at least the correct amount of water for your body weight. Take your body weight, round it upwards to the nearest 10, divide by 10 and add 2. This is the number of 250 ml glasses of water you should drink every day. If, for example, you weigh 76 kg, you should drink 10 glasses of water (80/10 + 2 = 10).

14. TAKE ESSENTIAL FATTY ACIDS

As the body does need certain types of fats to function, it's vital to take the correct amount of essential fatty acids in supplement form every day. These fatty acids are:

x   Omega 6 oils: Gamma-linolenic Acid (GLA), found in evening-primrose oil.
x   Omega 3 oils: Docosahexaenoic Acid (DHA) and Eicosapentaenoic Acid (EPA), found in fatty-fish oils.

You need these fatty acids to lose body fat and to improve insulin resistance. Without them, you may develop serious deficiency diseases. Ask your pharmacist, doctor or dietician to recommend the correct dosage for your needs, and remember to take your supplements every day.

15. EAT OAT BRAN

Oat bran, available in the cereal department of most supermarkets, lowers the GI score of almost everything you eat. In other words, it slows the rate at which sugars are released into the bloodstream. Adding a tablespoon or two of oat bran to cereals, muffins, home-baked bread, mashed potato and stews not only helps control blood sugar but also actively reduces cholesterol problems and increases the frequency of bowel movements.

16. EAT AS OFTEN AS YOU CAN

To maintain good blood-sugar levels and to prevent hunger, eat as often as you can. Remember that when you get hungry your body begins to auto-cannibalise its own muscle cells, which can slow the metabolism. You must keep your metabolism busy by giving it plenty of 'work' to do, especially if you choose the low-GI foods over the high ones.

17. EXERCISE REGULARLY

Exercise is imperative for achieving and maintaining good health. Regular weight-bearing exercise, in particular, will help build muscle mass and will mean that you see the results of the X Diet more quickly. If you are not in the habit of exercising, seek the help of a registered instructor or a biokineticist, who will work out the right exercise plan for your body and lifestyle.

18. FORBID 'DIET' FOOD

Make sure that your food does not resemble 'diet food'. Tasteless, unrewarding eating is not the key to slimming, no matter how pious it might make you feel! Try to aim for a joyous and sensuous taste experience at every meal. It is vitally important to enjoy your food, both physically and emotionally. If you eat like a martyr, many other mental and physiological complications will arise.

19. LAYER YOUR FOOD

By 'layer', I mean try to have a starter, a main course and a pudding-type food at every meal. These portions can be as big or small as you wish. By layering your meals, you will ensure that you are eating a good variety of foods, and that you never feel deprived. It also satisfies the most important factor in dietetics: a variety of foods. This will eliminate the need for any unnecessary and expensive multi-vitamins, because you will be getting more than the recommended daily allowance of micronutrients out of all the different and tasty combinations!

20. FOLLOW THE 'RULE OF SEVEN'

The backbone of good nutrition is variety. Try to eat at least seven different types of food with every meal. For a mid-afternoon snack, for example, you might eat the following: a few celery sticks with oil-free dressing, a muffin with fat-free cottage cheese and strawberry jam, a fat-free fruit yoghurt, a fresh, crispy apple and a large glass of water. By eating so many different foods, you will not only keep your tastebuds happy, but you'll also ensure a healthy colon and immune system.

21. ENJOY YOUR FOOD!

Food will always make you happy. It will always be there at celebrations. It will always be your comforter. It will always be your reward. It will always be associated with giving and nurturing. It will always be there. So enjoy it!

Important note

If you have a medical disorder, and you follow my guidelines without first consulting your doctor or a registered dietician, you run the risk of creating additional health problems. Everything that we put into our mouths affects every part of our bodies, and there are many people with physical anomalies that may either improve or worsen by following the X Diet.

I refer not only to serious medical conditions such as epilepsy, diabetes, heart disease, kidney disease, high blood pressure and clinical depression, but also those common health problems that on the surface seem to warrant little concern, such as heartburn, spastic colon, arthritis, gout and acne. If you suffer from any of these conditions, or any other illnesses or symptoms that may be of concern to you, you must consult a registered clinical dietician before embarking on a fat-free diet. He or she will combine the guidelines in this book with other dietetic advice specifically tailored to your particular condition.

fat-free cooking

So entrenched is the idea that everything we eat needs to be sautéed in butter or oil first, and enriched with cream after cooking, that it's hard to imagine that food will ever taste good without fat. Believe me, it will – and it does!

It's all a matter of technique. And the most important technique of all is...

THE DRY-FRY METHOD

I developed the dry-fry method in response to the common complaint that most savoury dishes taste unappealing if they don't include onions sizzled to a glossy-golden brown in oil or butter.

Think about it: virtually half the recipes in your average cookbook start with the words 'Fry the onions in butter or oil', so it's no wonder that many people associate fried onions so strongly with comforting home-cooked meals.

But a cornerstone of the X Diet is that all fat – whether it's olive oil, sunflower oil, pressed seed oils, butter, margarine, fish oil or a spray-on oil – is eliminated from the diet. Does this mean that food has to taste bland and look pallid?

No!

The dry-fry method results in onions that are golden brown, caramelised, succulent and packed with flavour, but there is no fat involved. It works best with onions because they are sugary and caramelise easily, but it can be used with great success to brown a variety of other firm vegetables, and to sear pieces of chicken and fish. It takes a little longer, admittedly, than simply throwing onions into hot oil, but the intense flavour and good colour of the end product make it worth the trouble.

Please note that dry-frying vegetables properly is pivotal to the success of many of the cooked dishes in this book, which is the reason I have described the method in such minute detail. Some people think that dry-frying means boiling in a little stock until soft. Never! If you do this, you will end up with soggy, transparent onions as a base for each meal, and after three weeks or so you will crave real, strong flavours. Follow the directions below carefully, and don't be tempted to hurry the process. Once you have perfected the method of 'sautéeing' onions and other veggies in this way, chances are you will never reach for the oil bottle again.

how to dry-fry onions

5 ml (1 tsp) stock powder
125 ml ($^1/_2$ cup) boiling water
125 ml ($^1/_2$ cup) white wine
250 ml (1 cup) very finely chopped onions

Combine stock powder, boiling water and wine in a small jug and stir until stock has dissolved. Heat a heavy-bottomed frying pan or saucepan and add onions. Using a wooden spoon, toss onions over a moderately high heat. Soon they will begin to stick, and a reddish-brown residue will appear on the bottom of the pan. Continue to cook for about 30–45 seconds after this residue appears, tossing the onions constantly, while they begin to stick. Pour about 2 tablespoons of the stock into the pan (any more will result in simmering, which we don't want). Stand back a little, as the liquid will send up a cloud of steam as it hits the hot pan. Briskly stir the onions as the stock bubbles furiously. When most of the liquid has evaporated, leaving a sticky sheen on the bottom of the pan, add another tiny amount of stock and repeat the process. Then repeat several more times. Keep the heat turned up so that the liquid keeps evaporating and the onions are not allowed to boil in it. When the onions are a rich and dark golden brown, add all the remaining stock and stir briskly to lift any residue off the bottom of the pan. Cover the pan and allow the onions to simmer for a few minutes. The stock in the pan should reduce to a thickish and glossy consistency as the onions caramelise. Now add any other ingredients specified in the recipe, such as green peppers, carrots, mushrooms, chicken breast pieces, prawns, and so on. You will find that these will colour easily as they cook in the rich, brown onion juices.

IMPORTANT POINTS ABOUT DRY-FRYING

x If you find that the onions are not turning a rich golden brown, it's probably because you are adding too much stock at a time. Remember that simmering water does not reach the same scorching temperature as steam! Try adding the liquid a tablespoon at a time until you have become accustomed to the browning technique. You should add only enough water to lift the onions and to create sufficient steam to brown them.

x If you have added too much liquid and find that the vegetables have started to simmer, wait until the liquid has completely evaporated, and the onions are sticking to the pan again, before adding any more.

x You do not need a non-stick frying pan, but your pan should have a heavy bottom. This technique will not damage the surface of your pots and they will clean very easily.

x Although onions work best because of their high sugar content, any non-watery vegetable can be successfully dry-fried. Leeks, peppers, garlic, spring onions, celery, carrots, turnips and parsnips produce particularly good results.

x If you are adapting a recipe that calls for chicken or seafood to be browned in fat as a starting point, simply dry-fry the pieces of chicken breast, fish or prawns exactly as you would onions. Although the pieces will initially stick quite fiercely to the bottom of the pan, they will lift away very easily as you add the liquid.

x If you're cooking a curry or a similarly spicy dish, put the ground spices into the dry frying pan first. Heat for a minute or so until the spices smell aromatic, then add the onions and start the dry-fry method. Adding sherry or coca cola to the dry-fry mixture will ensure that the spices 'open' (give out their aromas) sufficiently.

x Any vegetable that is to be dry-fried should be chopped rather more finely than you would usually chop it.

x You can use mushroom, chicken or vegetable stock powder, depending on the dish you're planning.

x Home-made vegetable stock makes all the difference to soups and stews *(see page 13)*.

x If you're planning a dish with a deep, rich colour, such as one containing mushrooms, spinach or butternut, use red wine instead of white. Although cheap wine will do, the finer the wine, the finer the taste.

x Beer and cider are also good for dry-frying.

x Don't worry about making everyone drunk when you cook with wine – the alcohol burns off during cooking. If you don't want to use alcohol, use grape or apple juice instead; the effect is just as good.

x Soy sauce and balsamic vinegar can be added to the stock and wine to create a deep rich colour and intense flavour.

fat-free cooking tips

CHOOSE THE RIGHT COOKWARE

Although it's not essential to have non-stick cookware, one or two really good items will make life a little easier. Commercial baking sprays are made with lecithin, a pure fat, so there are only a few recipes in this book that advise you to use baking spray, and all of them are delicate cakes that stick like the devil to the baking tin. Avoid baking sprays at all other times.

Parchment paper, available at kitchen shops, is very useful for baking ultra-sticky items such as meringues. Large paper muffin cases will also save you time and energy.

Here are some pieces of cookware you might consider buying:

x A heavy-bottomed frying pan with a tough non-stick surface. Invest in a really good one, as inexpensive Teflon-coated pans tend to scratch and peel within months.

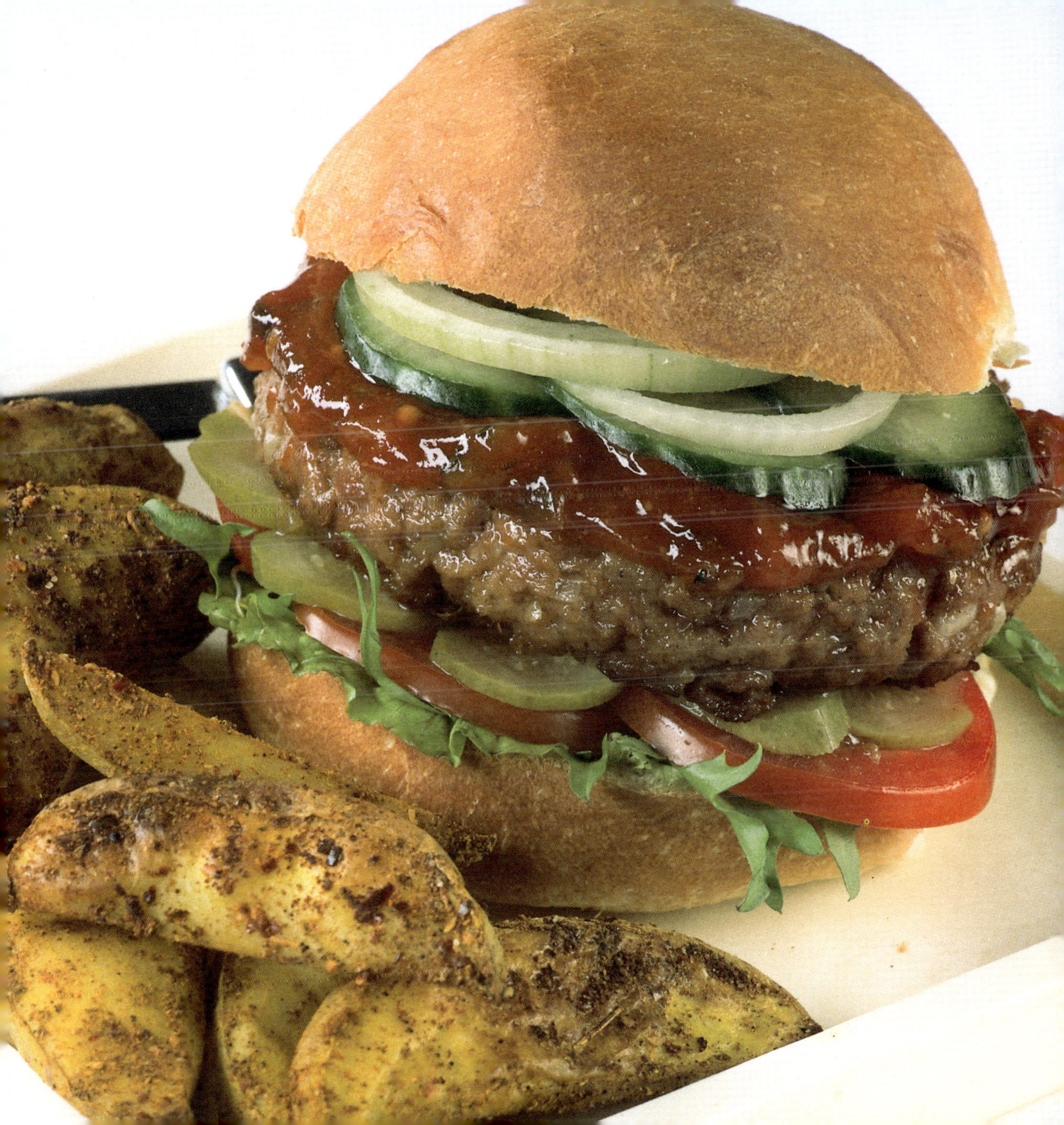

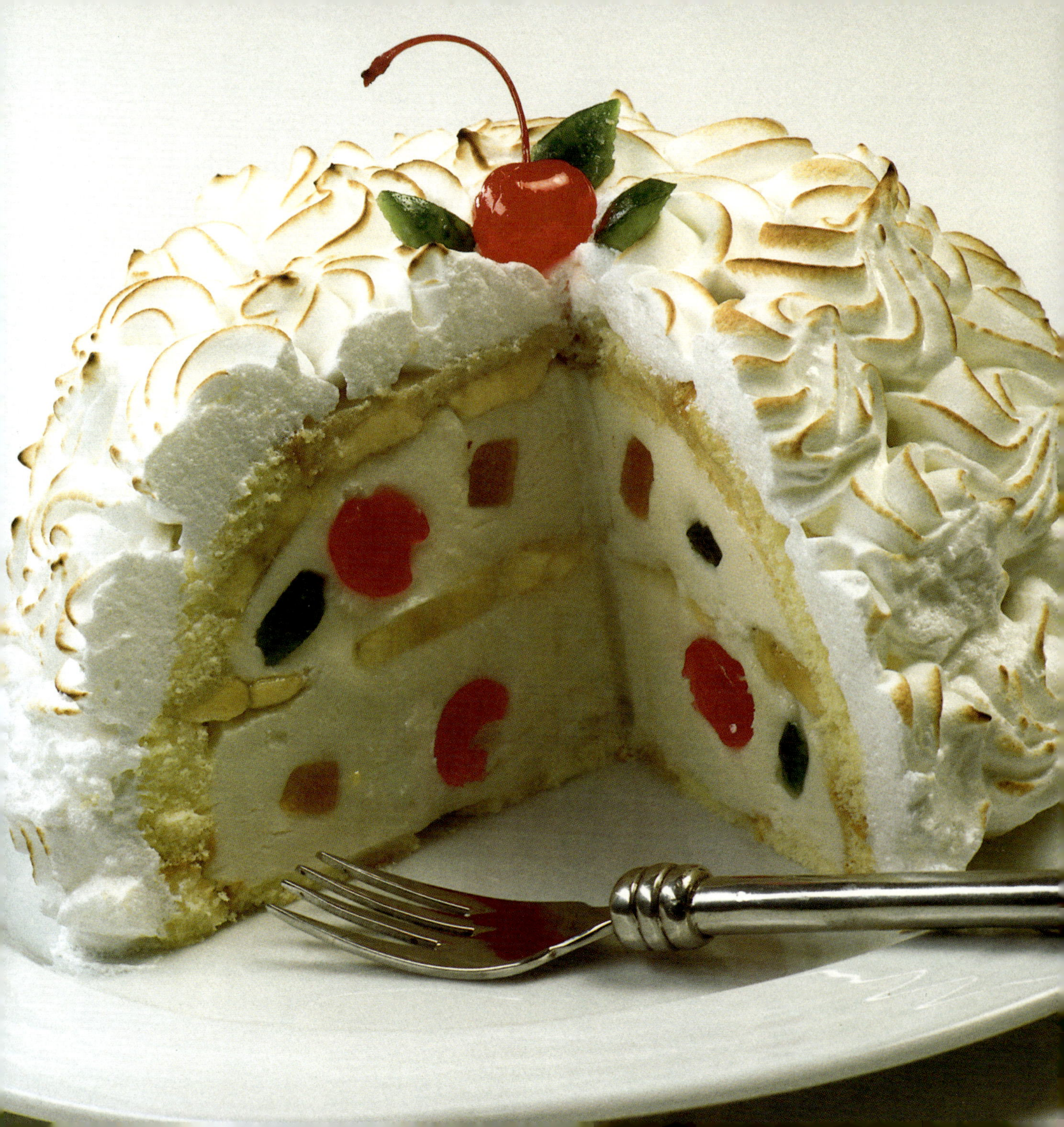

x A good non-stick baking sheet. This is a very useful item, especially when it comes to baking food that is traditionally deep-fried, such as crumbed fish, crumbed chicken breasts, fish cakes and potatoes.

x Non-stick baking tins. If you're planning to bake muffins frequently, a non-stick muffin pan is an excellent buy and will save you a good few minutes of digging and prising with a knife. If the muffins still stick a bit, use a plastic or rubber spatula to encircle and remove them without lifting the Teflon. A non-stick cake tin and/or loaf tin will be handy if you do a great deal of baking, and will obviate the need for you to use baking spray.

x A medium-sized, non-stick ovenproof dish with a tight-fitting lid is useful for casseroles and other oven-baked dishes, but not essential. I bake everything in my trusty old fireproof glass baking dishes, and I've never had a problem with food sticking.

BE LAVISH WITH YOUR FLAVOURS

There is no doubt that fat contributes a great deal of flavour and texture to the food that we eat, hence the popularity of greasy fast foods! Food cooked without fat can sometimes be bland, so it's a good idea to increase the quantity of herbs, spices and condiments. The more flavourful your food, the more it will resemble your usual way of eating, and the less likely you are to throw in the towel and wolf down a kilogram of hot greasy chips. On *page xvi* I've provided a list of herbs, spices and other flavouring agents that are very useful in fat-free cooking.

Here are some general tips for adding flavour to your cooking:

x Use spices. Powdered spices have a very short shelf-life. Buy fresh, whole spices. Roast them by heating a dry frying pan and toasting the spices for 1 minute, or until they release their fragrance. Grind them in a mortar and pestle, food processor or coffee grinder. Spices that cannot be bought whole, such as paprika and turmeric, should be stored in tightly sealed bottles in a dark cupboard. Supermarket spices tend to be very pricey (and are sometimes stale) so try to track down an Oriental spice dealer who sells whole spices in bulk. You'll be amazed at the difference in both price and freshness.

x Use herbs. Use fresh herbs in preference to dried herbs as often as possible. If you don't have a garden, grow a few pots of fresh herbs on a sunny windowsill. When replacing fresh herbs with dried, decrease the quantity as drying tends to concentrate the flavour of foods: 30 ml (1 tbsp) fresh chopped herbs is roughly equal to 5–10 ml (1–2 tsp) dried herbs. Much depends on the type of herb, the method of drying and how long it's been in your cupboard, so use your judgement.

x Freeze herbs and spices. Some fresh herbs can be successfully frozen. Parsley and chives generally keep quite well in the freezer: simply place the herbs in a polythene bag, seal tightly and freeze. Fresh coriander loses some of its flavour when frozen, but it's so convenient to have it in the freezer when you're making a curry and it's not in season. Chop up the leaves, put them in an ice cube tray and cover with water before freezing. Horseradish and fresh ginger also keep very well in the freezer. Wrap the roots in foil before freezing, and grate while still frozen. Whole peeled cloves of garlic and whole chillies may also be successfully frozen.

x Make your own spice mixtures. I have used bottled spices in the recipes to save time, but I think that home-made spice mixtures are infinitely preferable to supermarket brands. A small supply of home-made garam masala, for example, will make a real difference to your curries. Although recipes for garam masala abound, a good basic mixture consists of 5 ml (1 tsp) each of cumin seeds, coriander seeds, whole cloves and black peppercorns, 15 ml (1 tbsp) cardamom seeds, 1 dried red chilli, a quarter of a nutmeg, grated, and a 5 cm piece of cinnamon stick. Roast the spices, grind in a coffee grinder or mortar and pestle, sieve to remove husks and store in an airtight jar. You might also want to make up your own seasoning mixtures for braaiing and grilling food. A useful method is to save the spice bottles fitted with plastic grinders now available at supermarkets and to fill them with your own combinations of whole spices and dried herbs. For a basic braai spice, try combining equal quantities of chilli flakes, paprika, cumin, cloves, cardamom, garlic flakes, peppercorns and oregano. And while you're about it, why not make your own seasoned salt by pounding dried herbs and spices with coarse sea salt or rock salt?

x Don't skimp on condiments. There is a vast difference between a cheap, salty soy sauce coloured with caramel and a thick Japanese soy sauce brewed from only wheat, soya beans and water, just as there is a difference between aged balsamic vinegar and cheap spirit vinegar. If a recipe calls for white wine, use a decent one and you'll notice the difference in the final product. Good condiments are more expensive, but they go a long way.

x Taste and taste again. I've put a great deal of emphasis on flavour in this book because I believe it's so important that fat-free food should taste really good. Taste the food as you go along, and feel free to increase the specified amounts of herbs, spices and flavourings to suit yourself.

DON'T GIVE UP BAKING

It's hard to imagine baking anything at all without lavish amounts of butter, lard or margarine, but let me assure you that there are many ways to cook delicious cakes, muffins and breads without using fat. (There are, of course, exceptions. You can't make shortcrust pastry without fat, and croissants are out of the question!)

One technique is to use fat-free dairy products, such as yoghurt and cottage cheese to add moistness and flavour. Even more effective is to use fruit purées in place of fat, in a 1:1 proportion (that is, one cup of purée to each cup of fat called for in the recipe). Apple purée and mashed banana are the most commonly used fruit purées in fat-free baking, but you can also use the following:

x Bottled baby foods made of puréed fruits, such as pear, peach and apricot. Bottled puréed prunes are particularly delicious as they have a lovely flavour and a rich, dark colour.

x Bottled apple sauce.

x Tinned pie apples. Tinned pears, guavas, apricots and peaches can also be used. Simply place in the food processor and whiz to a purée.

x Stewed fresh apples. Mix together sugar and water to make a light syrup and simmer until sugar dissolves. Cut up a few apples and add to the syrup. Simmer until the apples are very tender, then place in the goblet of a food processor or blender and process to a coarse purée. There is no need to peel the apples, as the peel adds flavour and texture to the purée.

x Soaked dried fruit, such as sultanas, dried apricots, prunes and figs. Cover the fruit with hot rooibos tea or cold orange juice and soak until soft and plump. Liquidise to a smooth purée, adding more water if the texture is too thick.

TRY NEW FOOD PRODUCTS

Take a spin around a good supermarket, reading the labels carefully, and you'll be amazed at the diversity of fat-free products now available. For some reason, most food manufacturers in this country haven't twigged on to the idea of actually advertising the fact that their products are exceptionally low in fat, so it's important to do a little sleuthing of your own.

A rule of thumb with label-reading is never to take anything for granted. As I pointed out at great length in my book *The X Diet*, products you assume are fat free, or which claim to be very low in fat, are probably not. And delicious foods that you thought must contain loads of fat actually don't. A good example is Nesquick chocolate-flavoured milk mix, which is fat free. Hershey's chocolate syrup and their instant vanilla and chocolate puddings are also fat free (provided that they are made up with fat-free milk). Creamed sweetcorn is fat free, and so are baked beans in tomato sauce. Custard powder is fat free. Many brands of 'cook-in' sauces designed for pouring over chicken contain less than 3 g of fat per 100 g of product. Most chutneys, ketchups, soya sauces and American mustards are also fat free. Always read the label on any pre-prepared foods you are thinking of buying; it doesn't take long to work out the fat content of a product, and it doesn't require a degree in maths!

SEXY BOTTLES AND TINS

Here are some fabulous tinned and bottled products that are fat-free. Keep a supply of them on hand at all times and you'll never be at a loss for what to cook.

- tuna in brine
- smoked mussels in brine
- clams in brine
- shrimps in brine
- creamed and whole-kernel sweetcorn
- baby sweetcorn
- kidney beans
- butter beans
- lentils
- baked beans in tomato sauce
- chickpeas
- capers in brine
- green peppercorns in brine
- pimentos
- gherkins
- pickled onions
- peeled tomatoes, whole or chopped
- tomato and onion mix
- preserved vine leaves
- asparagus spears
- artichoke hearts
- bamboo shoots
- peaches, pears, guavas, litchis, mandarins, blueberries, pineapple chunks, etc
- fat-free rice pudding
- jams
- fruit jellies
- honey
- molasses
- golden syrup
- chocolate syrup
- Denny Condensed Cream of Mushroom Soup

SEXY DRIED GOODS

- soft brown sugar
- raisins and sultanas
- dried fruit
- dates
- phyllo pastry
- sun-dried tomatoes (not in oil)
- dried wild mushrooms
- All-Bran flakes
- oat bran
- rolled oats
- custard powder
- powdered or flaked mashed potato mix
- pasta
- pasta-in-sauce (Tuna-Mate)
- Kellogg's Cornflakes Crumbs
- fat-free milk powder
- fat-free instant puddings
- jelly powder

SEXY FLAVOURINGS AND CONDIMENTS

All the following flavouring agents are free of fat and will go a long way towards making the food you cook taste quite delicious. Use them with abandon!

- fresh or dried herbs
- chilli flakes
- garlic flakes
- whole spices: coriander, cumin, cardamom, fenugreek, nutmeg, mustard seed, caraway, etc
- garam masala
- ground spices: turmeric, paprika, ginger, cinnamon, cayenne pepper, etc
- curry powder: mild, medium or hot and curry pastes
- preserved lemon grass, ginger, etc
- peppercorns
- seasoned sea salt and rock salt
- stock powder: chicken, mushroom and vegetable
- tomato paste, purée and concentrate
- wine, sherry, brandy, vodka
- rice wine
- dark soy sauce
- coconut, almond, coffee and vanilla essence
- vanilla pods
- mustards: Dijon, wholegrain, American, English, mustard seeds, etc
- vinegars: balsamic, cider, white wine, etc
- Tabasco, Worcestershire and HP Sauce
- Bovril or Marmite
- tomato sauce and chutneys
- Piccalilli and Branston Pickle
- Bisto gravy powder
- Royco Brown Onion Soup
- Cubb's Chip Dips (although they contain more than 3% fat, when mixed with fat-free cottage cheese or fat-free milk they act like a stock, thereby reducing the amount of fat per 100 g serving of the mix.

starters

Starters are a super way to set the tone for a meal, and to whet the appetite of keen and hungry guests. But starters are too often seen as something to leave out if you are to be healthy because they are usually full of the wrong things. It is when patients mention that they 'wouldn't make their guests eat fat-free food', that I know they do not know the potential of what honest culinary desires can create with mother nature! With my recipes, the host or hostess no longer has to sit and 'be strong' whilst everyone else enjoys what is supposed to be a special introduction to a special evening. If your guests can tell that these starters are fat free, chances are they have the X Diet cookbook, too!

Whether you're making nibbles to accompany the rugby before the braai begins (such as Boerewors with Creamy Mediterranean Salsa), or a delectable dish served on your best china (Asparagus with Tangy Sauce), you can now eat with your friends and excite those tastebuds as much as a chef deserves! Even the hands-on snacks before dinner show that the X Diet is associated with enjoyment and sociability, and not with hunger pangs!

asparagus with tangy sauce

This aristocratic vegetable brings a touch of class to any dinner table. Serve chilled, with no more than this tangy warm sauce to bring out its flavour.

24 fresh, green asparagus tips
juice of 2 lemons
40 ml (2 heaped tbsp) capers in vinegar, drained
4 medium-sized gherkins
10 ml (2 tsp) finely chopped onion
10 ml (2 tsp) sugar
juice of 1 lemon
250 ml (1 cup) fat-free plain yoghurt
60 ml (4 tbsp) cider vinegar
6 fresh mint leaves

To blanch the asparagus, bring a saucepan of salted water to the boil. As soon as the water is boiling vigorously, tip in all of the asparagus. Cook for 2 - 5 minutes, depending on the thickness of the tips, until just tender. Remove from the heat, drain and plunge immediately into a bowl of iced water. Put the asparagus, still in the iced water, into the refrigerator. Put all of the remaining ingredients into a food processor or blender and process until smooth. Put into a saucepan. Over a low heat, gently warm the yoghurt mixture until skin temperature (do not heat it too quickly or it will separate). Drain the asparagus and serve with the warm sauce.

Serves 4

SEXY OPTIONS

This recipe can be 'reversed' if you like, with a chilled sauce and piping hot asparagus. Follow the recipe as above (still plunging the asparagus into iced water) but chill the sauce instead of warming it. Just before serving, plunge the asparagus into boiling water for 30 seconds, to reheat. However you serve this dish, it is important to put the asparagus into iced water after cooking as this ensures it retains its bright green colour.

prawn and cucumber mousse

Here's a refreshing starter with a creamy texture and delicate flavour, ideal for a dinner party on a warm summer evening.

$1/2$ English cucumber
125 ml ($1/2$ cup) fat-free cottage cheese
185 ml ($3/4$ cup) fat-free plain yoghurt
2 ml ($1/2$ tsp) chicken stock powder
125 ml ($1/2$ cup) boiling water
15 ml (1 tbsp) gelatine
250 ml (1 cup) cooked, shelled prawns or shrimps tinned in brine
60 ml (4 tbsp) lemon juice
salt and milled black pepper
fat-free plain yoghurt, chopped fresh dill and cayenne pepper, to serve

Peel and coarsely grate the cucumber. Put into a sieve, sprinkle with salt and leave to drain for 30 minutes. Beat together the cottage cheese and yoghurt until smooth. Dissolve the stock powder in the boiling water. Add the gelatine to the stock mixture and stir well until dissolved. Briefly rinse cucumber then squeeze out the excess moisture by pressing down on it with the back of a saucer or small plate. Gently mix together all the ingredients. Pour into 4 individual ramekins or miniature fish moulds and chill overnight, or for at least 4 hours, until set. Turn out onto serving plates, spoon some yoghurt around and sprinkle with chopped dill and cayenne pepper.

Serves 4

SEXY OPTIONS

Garnish each mousse with a whole large prawn and/or a little pile of caviar.

spicy bean samoosas

These Indian delicacies are traditionally deep-fried, but baking them in the oven gives just as good results. Serve as finger food, with a bowl of fruity chutney or fat-free plain yoghurt for dipping them in.

2 onions, chopped
1 clove garlic, peeled and crushed
15 ml (1 tbsp) curry powder (mild, medium or hot, according to your tastes)
5 ml (1 tsp) turmeric
10 ml (2 tsp) ground coriander
5 ml (1 tsp) salt
5 ml (1 tsp) ginger paste
3 green chillies, de-seeded and finely chopped
30 ml (2 tbsp) garam masala
2 tins (420 g each) kidney beans, rinsed and drained
1 tin (420 g) butter beans, rinsed and drained
1 packet (500 g) phyllo pastry
1 egg white, lightly beaten
30 ml (2 tbsp) fat-free milk
fresh coriander sprigs
fruity chutney and fat-free plain yoghurt, to serve

Dry-fry the onions *(see page xi)* with the garlic, curry powder, turmeric, ground coriander, salt, ginger paste and chillies until golden brown and aromatic. Put the onion mixture in a blender or food processor with the garam masala, kidney beans and butter beans and process until smooth. Set aside. Preheat oven to 220 °C. Cut the phyllo pastry into 24 strips, 5 x 30 cm. Mix together the egg white and milk. Taking one strip of pastry at a time, lightly brush with the egg white mixture, then fold the bottom right hand corner over to the long side on the left, so that there is a triangle of pastry at the bottom of the strip. Fold this triangle up again, to form a small pocket. Carefully fill the pocket with about a teaspoonful of the bean filling. Continue folding the triangle until you get to the end of the strip and the filling is completely enclosed. Brush the last flap with a little of the egg white mixture and press gently to secure. Repeat this with each pastry strip. Arrange the finished samoosas on a non-stick baking sheet, brush the tops with egg white mixture and bake for about 15 minutes, or until the phyllo pastry is crisp and browning at the edges. Garnish with fresh coriander sprigs and serve hot, with fruity chutney or fat-free plain yoghurt for dipping.

Makes 24 small samoosas

COOK'S TIPS

x *Phyllo pastry is the only kind of pastry that is low in fat. It is always rolled into wafer-thin sheets that crisp beautifully when cooked. Ready-made and ready-rolled phyllo is sold fresh or frozen in large supermarkets or delicatessens. Phyllo pastry dries out very quickly, so when you are working with it take one sheet at a time and keep the rest covered with a damp tea towel.*

roasted garlic with bagel melbas

Don't be dismayed if your guests are horrified at the thought of eating whole garlic cloves! Once you've coaxed them into trying this delicious starter, they'll be hooked for life!

4 whole bulbs garlic
4 bagels, sliced as thinly as possible

Preheat oven to 120 °C. Put the whole garlic bulbs, with the skin still on, on a baking tray and roast for 30 minutes. Put the bagel slices on another baking tray and bake along with the garlic for 30 minutes. To serve, arrange the whole garlic bulbs and bagel slices on warmed serving plates. To eat, gently break off each garlic clove and press between the fingers, until the soft, buttery garlic oozes out of the skin and on to the bagel melba. Grind coarse sea salt over the top and devour!

Serves 4

COOK'S TIPS

x *It's best to use bagels that are a day or two old – they're much easier to slice.*

tzatziki

This wonderfully versatile dish can be found in various guises in many parts of the world. Like hummus, it's also great served with pita wedges. Why not spoil your guests and serve them both dips?

1 large English cucumber
10 ml (2 tsp) salt
500 ml (2 cups) fat-free plain yoghurt
4 cloves garlic, peeled and crushed
15 ml (1 tbsp) finely chopped fresh coriander
15 ml (1 tbsp) finely chopped fresh mint
juice of 2 lemons
milled black pepper

Wash cucumber well but do not peel. Grate coarsely and tip pulp into a sieve. Sprinkle with salt and allow to drain for 30 minutes. Whisk together yoghurt, garlic, coriander, mint, lemon juice and pepper. Briefly rinse cucumber under running water and squeeze out all excess moisture by pressing down with the back of a small plate or saucer. Tip cucumber onto a clean tea towel and pat dry. Put cucumber in a bowl, add yoghurt mixture and stir well. Serve chilled, with pita wedges or crudités *(see Sexy options, page 6)*.

COOK'S TIPS

x Try to find a thick yoghurt to use in Tzatziki, because even the most thoroughly drained cucumber will eventually 'leak'. Thicken yoghurt yourself by lining a sieve with clean cheesecloth or a double layer of paper towel. Tip the yoghurt into the sieve and allow to drain over the sink for at least 2 hours. The longer you leave it, the thicker the resulting 'cheese' left behind in the sieve.

SEXY OPTIONS

Convert Tzatziki into a delicious cold Persian Soup by thinning it down to pouring consistency with fat-free milk or fat-free plain yoghurt. Stir in 5 ml (1 tsp) sugar, 30 ml (2 tbsp) tarragon vinegar and a handful of chopped fresh dill.

mediterranean garlic musssels

Seafood always makes a good starter – it's not too filling and tasty enough to get those tastebuds tingling. Try these juicy mussels with their crisp, garlic-flavoured topping.

16 fresh mussels
2 whole bulbs garlic
1 slice bread, made into breadcrumbs
125 ml ($1/2$ cup) white wine
125 ml ($1/2$ cup) chopped fresh parsley
salt

Soak the mussels in salted water for $1 1/2$ hours. Scrub clean and rinse well *(see Cook's tips, page 50)*. Preheat oven to 120 °C. Put the garlic bulbs on a baking tray and roast for 1 hour. Increase the oven temperature to 200 °C. Put the mussels on a baking tray and bake for about 10 minutes, until the shells have opened. Discard the empty shell halves, and remove the 'beards'. Arrange in a single layer on a baking tray. Meanwhile, squeeze each garlic clove into a bowl, using your fingers to press the soft, hot garlic out of the skin. (Use some folded kitchen paper to protect your fingers from the heat.) Add the breadcrumbs, wine, parsley and salt to the garlic and mix well to combine. Put about a teaspoonful of the garlic mixture on top of each mussel. Return the mussels to the oven and bake until the sauce begins to bubble. Serve hot, with slices of fresh brown bread.

Serves 4

prawn spring rolls

If you're planning a meal with an Oriental theme, such as Chinese Chicken *(see page 69)*, then here's the ideal starter – rolls of crisp, golden pastry with a succulent filling of prawns and vegetables.

10 large raw prawns, shelled
1 onion, finely chopped
2 spring onions, sliced (including green parts)
4 cloves garlic, peeled and crushed
30 ml (2 tbsp) soft brown sugar
10 ml (2 tsp) ground ginger
60 ml (4 tbsp) sherry
5 carrots, grated
½ head red cabbage, finely shredded
250 ml (1 cup) bean sprouts
juice of 2 lemons mixed with 125 ml (½ cup) water
125 ml (½ cup) soy sauce
1 packet (500 g) phyllo pastry (see Cook's tips, page 3)
1 egg white, lightly beaten
60 ml (4 tbsp) fat-free milk
lemon wedges, soy sauce and sweet and sour sauce, to serve

Cook the prawns in boiling salted water for 1 minute. Drain and set aside. Dry-fry the onions, spring onions, garlic, sugar and ground ginger *(see page xi)*. Add the sherry and the remaining vegetables. Cover and simmer gently for 1–2 minutes, stirring in the lemon juice and water mixture when the vegetables begin to stick. Add the prawns to the pan. Gradually stir in the soy sauce, adding just enough to evenly coat the vegetables and prawns without making the sauce too dark. Remove from the heat and leave to cool. Preheat oven to 180 °C. Cut the phyllo pastry into 20 strips, 10 x 30 cm . Mix together the egg white and the milk. To make each spring roll, take one phyllo strip at a time and lightly brush with the egg white mixture. Put 2-3 tablespoons of the vegetable mixture, including 1 prawn, lengthways along the centre of the pastry strip, leaving about 5 cm at each end. Fold the outer flaps of pastry over the filling, and then fold the top and the bottom flaps over each other. Brush another strip of phyllo with the egg white mixture and put the filled pastry at one end. Carefully roll it up in the pastry. Moisten the end of the roll, and press gently to secure. Repeat to make 10 rolls. Put on a baking tray, brush the tops with egg white mixture and bake for about 15 minutes, until the phyllo pastry is crisp and browning at the edges. Serve hot with lemon wedges and little bowls of soy sauce and sweet and sour sauce for dipping.

Makes 10 spring rolls

garlic bread

No-one can resist garlic bread, and now you don't even have to try — here's the long-awaited fat-free version.

1 baguette
6 cloves garlic, peeled
250 ml (1 cup) buttermilk or fat-free plain yoghurt
salt and milled black pepper

Preheat oven to 180 °C. Bake the garlic cloves for 45 minutes, until soft. Meanwhile, slice the baguette without cutting all the way through. Put the garlic into a bowl and mash until smooth. Stir in the buttermilk or yoghurt and salt and pepper. Put about 2 tablespoons of the mixture into each cut in the bread. Wrap in foil and bake at 180 °C for 20 minutes, or until crust is crispy.

SEXY OPTIONS

For a herby garlic bread, add 30 ml (2 tbsp) each of chopped fresh parsley and shredded basil leaves to the garlic mixture.

boerewors with tomato and chilli salsa

Traditional boerewors is loaded with enough fats to last a lifetime, but make friends with your local butcher and, after much persuasion, you'll have your own custom-made, fat-free boerewors.

4 long strips (about 100 g) fat-free boerewors (see Cook's tips)

TOMATO AND CHILLI SALSA
8 sun-dried tomatoes
20 ml (4 tsp) sugar
1 fresh green chilli, de-seeded and chopped
2 cloves garlic, peeled and crushed
30 ml (2 tbsp) grated fresh ginger
juice of 1 lemon
15 ml (1 tbsp) white wine vinegar
salt and milled black pepper
2 handfuls fresh basil
250 ml (1 cup) fat-free plain yoghurt

To make the salsa, put the sun-dried tomatoes and 5 ml (1 tsp) sugar in boiling water and soak for 30 minutes, until soft. Drain the tomatoes and put in a food processor or blender with all the remaining ingredients and process until smooth. Transfer to a serving bowl and chill. Meanwhile, braai the boerewors over hot coals, turning regularly, for 5 - 10 minutes. Serve hot with the chilled salsa.

Serves 4

COOK'S TIPS

x To get your fat-free boerewors, be sure to find a butcher you trust, because it took three attempts to get mine to use the right things (he was afraid of dryness). Tell your butcher to use only ostrich fillet, minced, with nothing added at all. Then to add the 'rusk' that is normally used for boerewors. The butcher will be anxious to add some fat, to give the right texture, but emphasise that this is exactly how you want it made. The sausage will only become dry if you overcook it, or don't have a sauce such as the one here to smother it with!

hummus with pita wedges

A deliciously rich dip, popular in many Mediterranean countries. The pita wedges are a fat-free alternative to crisps, and so simple to make.

1 tin (400 g) chickpeas, rinsed and drained
juice of 1 lemon
10 ml (2 tsp) salt
5 ml (1 tsp) milled black pepper
2 ml ($^1/_2$ tsp) ground coriander
3 cloves garlic, peeled and crushed
125 ml ($^1/_2$ cup) fat-free plain yoghurt
4 pita breads
fresh coriander sprigs

Put all the ingredients except pita breads and coriander sprigs into a blender or food processor and process until smooth. Transfer to a serving bowl and chill. Preheat oven to 180 °C. Cut each pita bread into quarters, to give 16 wedges in total. Arrange the wedges in a single layer on a baking tray and bake for about 15 minutes, until crisp. Garnish the chilled hummus with coriander sprigs and serve with the hot pita wedges.

Serves 4

SEXY OPTIONS

Sprinkle the pita wedges with paprika (for a mildly spicy taste) or cayenne pepper (for a real bite) before baking.

Give your guests a selection of crudités (crisp raw vegetables) for dipping instead of the pita wedges. Strips of red, green and yellow peppers, celery, carrot and cucumber make a colourful display.

soups

*T*he easiest way to add these incredibly important vitamins and minerals to your diet is in the form of soups. I can imagine your groans, and complaints of not having the time to make soup every day! Don't worry, if you follow some simple rules you'll soon get used to a fabulous three-course meal every night with hardly any effort at all – believe me! And anyway, I can't think of anything nicer than to invite some friends around for a dinner party and start with a cold summer white gazpacho or a rich black mushroom soup. No-one will refuse such temptations, especially not the cook trying to lose weight! Just remember these points:

1. Always keep the following stocked in your kitchen: vegetable stock, onions, celery, potatoes, carrots, pumpkin, butternut, broccoli, spinach, watercress or beetroot.
2. Make a large amount of soup each time, and freeze the surplus in convenient amounts – whatever's best for your family. This way, you will only have to cook a few times, and have soups for most other meals ready in a matter of minutes.
3. Remember that the soup recipes are not long and laborious. I am a working woman too!
4. Remember how important these soups are to providing the special veggies that are a crucial part of this diet. Especially when we make meals that don't normally warrant a side-serving of vegetables, such as pasta, what better than a piping hot butternut soup to start with?

But also remember, vegetable soups are not food! If you only have a thick broccoli soup for lunch, it is like giving your car all the washing and shining it needs to stay looking good, but no petrol! These are a lovely way to 'polish' your carbohydrate-rich meals, not replace them!

Vegetable, chicken or mushroom stock powder can be used in the recipes in this chapter. Many stock powders contain more than 3 g of fat per 100 g serving, but because only a small amount is used in soups, it's acceptable to break the 'rule'.

clam chowder

This mildly spicy soup makes a wonderful fat-free starter for a dinner party.

1 onion, chopped
5 ml (1 tsp) chilli powder
375 ml (1½ cups) frozen sweetcorn kernels
2 cloves garlic, peeled and crushed
250 ml (1 cup) frozen peas
1 packet Knorr Vegetable Soup powder
stock made with 875 ml (3½ cups) boiling water and 15 ml (1 tbsp) stock powder
12 frozen smoked clams in their shells (see Cook's tips)
salt and milled black pepper

Dry-fry onion and chilli powder *(see page xi)*. When onion is soft and golden, add sweetcorn, garlic, peas and vegetable soup powder. Stir well, then gradually add hot stock, stirring briskly between each addition to prevent lumps forming. Bring to the boil, stirring constantly, then reduce heat, cover and simmer until thick (about 10 minutes). Just before serving, add clams in their shells. Season with salt and pepper. Heat gently for 3 minutes. Serve hot.

Serves 4

COOK'S TIPS

x *Frozen smoked clams are available from good fishmongers.*

x *If you can't find clams, use frozen mussels in their shells or smoked mussels canned in brine.*

x *For a creamier result, make up the stock with half fat-free milk and half water.*

curried parsnip and apple soup
(See opposite)
Parsnips are not a commonly used ingredient in this country, which is a pity, as they have wonderful, earthy flavours.

6 cardamom pods
7 ml (1 heaped tsp) cumin seeds
7 ml (1 heaped tsp) coriander seeds
1 onion, chopped
5 ml (1 tsp) turmeric
5 ml (1 tsp) ground ginger
2 cloves garlic, peeled and crushed
750 ml (3 cups) peeled, sliced parsnips
stock made with 875 ml (3½ cups) boiling water and 10 ml (2 tsp) stock powder
1 apple
salt and milled black pepper
Parsnip Crisps (see Sexy options), *to serve*

Open cardamom pods, remove black seeds and discard husks. Heat a dry frying pan and heat cardamom seeds, cumin seeds and coriander seeds for a few minutes, or until seeds begin to crackle and release their aromas. Grind finely ina mortar and pestle and reserve. Dry-fry onion *(see page xi)* over a low heat. When onion is golden brown, add reserved spice mixture, turmeric, ground ginger and garlic and cook for a further 5 minutes. Add parsnips and stock, lower heat, cover and simmer gently for 1 hour. Liquidise soup in a blender or food processor, return to rinsed-out pot and reheat. While soup is warming, peel and grate the apple. Stir into soup and allow to simmer for another 2 - 3 minutes. Season to taste. Serve hot with Parsnip Crisps.

Serves 6

SEXY OPTIONS

To make Parsnip Crisps, peel several medium-sized parsnips and slice into very thin discs. Place on a baking sheet, sprinkle with seasoned sea salt and bake at 200°C for about 45 minutes until crisp and golden brown.

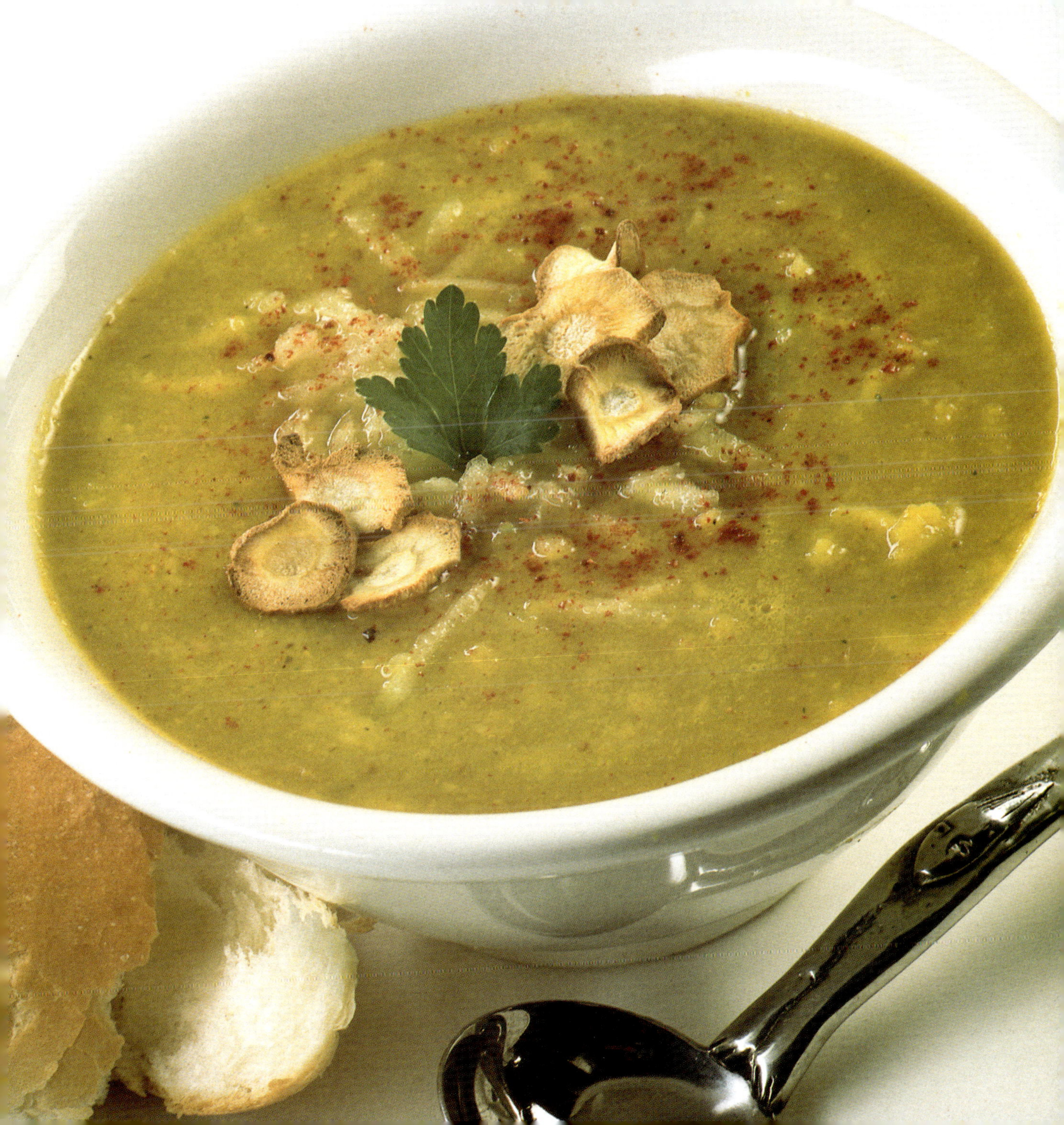

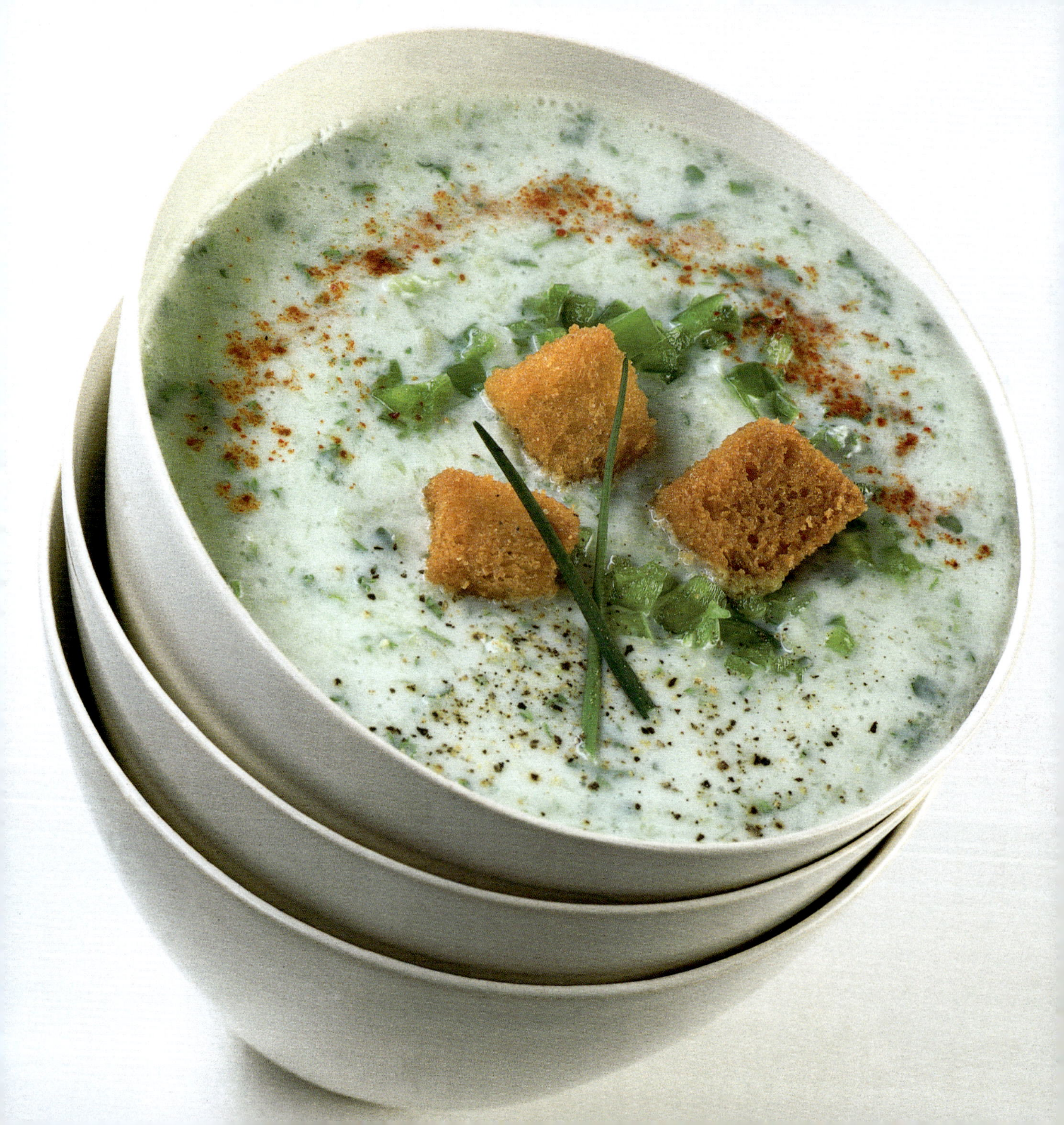

asparagus and artichoke soup

This delicate soup is the perfect prelude to a richly flavoured main course.

1 onion, finely chopped
5 ml (1 tsp) dried marjoram
10 ml (2 tsp) white sugar
20 ml (4 tsp) cornflour
125 ml (½ cup) fat-free milk
125 ml (½ cup) buttermilk
5 ml (1 tsp) chicken stock powder
15 ml (1 tbsp) sherry
15 ml (1 tbsp) white wine vinegar
1 tin (400 g) asparagus spears, plus their juice
1 tin (400 g) artichoke bottoms, plus their juice
salt and milled black pepper

Dry-fry onion, marjoram and sugar (see page xi) until onion is soft and transparent. Mix the cornflour with a little milk to make a smooth paste, then add to soup along with remaining milk, buttermilk, stock powder, sherry and wine vinegar. Add the asparagus spears and artichoke bottoms, plus the juice from the tins. Simmer, stirring constantly, until thickened. Liquidise soup in a blender or food processor, return to rinsed-out pot and reheat. Season with salt and pepper and serve hot.

Serves 4

SEXY OPTIONS

Make a soup from fresh asparagus when it's in season. Omit the artichoke bottoms and use 1 large bunch of asparagus and 500 ml (2 cups) stock. Chop and add to the pan after dry-frying the onions. Simmer until tender (about 20 minutes). Add the cornflour, etc and proceed with the recipe above.

white gazpacho

(See opposite)
Try this interesting variation on the classic cold Spanish soup.

2 English cucumbers, peeled and cubed
1 small bunch spring onions, chopped
1 green pepper, chopped
45 ml (3 tbsp) chopped fresh parsley
1 clove garlic, peeled and crushed
15 ml (1 tbsp) lemon juice
10 ml (2 tsp) sugar
500 ml (2 cups) fat-free plain yoghurt
15 ml (1 tbsp) vegetable or chicken stock powder
500 ml (2 cups) iced water
salt and milled black pepper

TOPPINGS
chopped fresh coriander or parsley
finely chopped green pepper
finely chopped cucumber
chopped spring onions
Crispy Croûtons (see Sexy options, page 12)

Put cucumber, spring onions, green pepper, parsley, garlic, lemon juice, sugar, yoghurt, stock powder and half the water into a blender or food processor and liquidise to a fairly coarse purée. Pour into a bowl and whisk in enough of the remaining water to achieve desired consistency. Season with salt and pepper then chill. Serve in iced bowls, and pass around the chopped vegetables, herbs and croûtons in separate bowls.

Serves 4

COOK'S TIPS

x If you prefer a thicker soup, soak a slice of white bread in iced water for a few minutes, squeeze dry and liquidise along with the soup.

x If you don't have time to cool the soup thoroughly, add a handful of crushed ice to each serving.

mexican corn soup

This soup is astonishingly quick to make, yet is so rich and flavourful that it tastes as if hours went into its preparation.

1 l (4 cups) frozen sweetcorn kernels
250 ml (1 cup) hot water
10 ml (2 tsp) chicken stock powder
2 cloves garlic, peeled
500 ml (2 cups) fat-free milk
125 ml ($1/2$ cup) white wine
5 ml (1 tsp) dried oregano
5 ml (1 tsp) chilli flakes (optional)
salt and milled black pepper

TOPPINGS
finely chopped spring onions
finely chopped fresh coriander
peeled, de-seeded and finely chopped tomatoes
de-seeded and finely chopped fresh green chillies
fat-free plain yoghurt

Put sweetcorn kernels (no need to thaw first), water, stock powder and garlic into a food processor fitted with a metal blade and liquidise to form a thick, smooth purée. Pour the purée into a large saucepan and whisk in milk, wine, oregano, chilli flakes and salt and pepper. Bring to the boil, stirring constantly. Cover and simmer for 10 minutes. If soup seems too thick, add a little hot water. Serve piping hot, and pass round the toppings in separate small bowls.

Serves 4

COOK'S TIPS

x Tinned sweetcorn (creamed or whole kernel) may be used in place of frozen kernels.

x If you prefer a chunkier soup, reserve 250 ml (1 cup) of whole kernels and add to soup after it has been liquidised.

basic vegetable soup

This thick, wholesome vegetable soup is quick and easy to prepare and makes a lovely lunch or light supper. You can use this recipe as a basis for a variety of tasty vegetable soups (see Sexy Options).

2 large potatoes, peeled and cubed
1 onion, chopped
3 ribs celery, including the tops, sliced
1 small bunch parsley
stock made with 1 litre (4 cups) boiling water and 20 ml (4 tsp) stock powder
500 ml (2 cups) seasonal vegetables (see Sexy Options)
salt and milled black pepper

Put potatoes, onion, celery and parsley in a large pot and cover with stock. Bring to the boil, then reduce heat, cover and simmer until potatoes are tender (about 25 minutes). Add seasonal vegetables, cover and simmer for a further 10 - 15 minutes, or until the vegetables are tender but not falling apart. Liquidise soup in a blender or food processor, return to rinsed-out pot and reheat. Season with salt and pepper and serve piping hot.

Serves 4

SEXY OPTIONS

Any seasonal vegetables can be added to basic Vegetable Soup. The following work well: butternut, pumpkin, parsnips, turnips, baby marrows, cauliflower and broccoli. Chop or cube as necessary.

fruity butternut soup

A rich and nourishing winter soup that's ideal for feeding a crowd. Serve with plenty of hot crusty bread.

2 onions, chopped
500 ml (2 cups) cubed butternut
stock made with 625 ml (2½ cups) boiling water and 10 ml (2 tsp) vegetable stock powder
1 Granny Smith apple, peeled and cubed
5 ml (1 tsp) mild curry powder, or to taste
1 ml (¼ tsp) freshly grated nutmeg
15 ml (1 tbsp) cornflour
375 ml (1½ cups) fat-free milk
finely grated zest and juice of 1 orange
salt and milled black pepper
125 ml (½ cup) fat-free plain yoghurt
15 ml (1 tbsp) chopped fresh parsley

Dry-fry onions *(see page xi)* until soft and golden. Add butternut and cook, stirring occasionally, until butternut begins to soften slightly. Add stock, apple, curry powder and nutmeg. Reduce heat, cover and simmer until butternut is very tender. Put cornflour in a teacup, add just enough of the milk to cover and stir to make a very smooth paste. Add flour paste to pot along with remaining milk and cook over a gentle heat, stirring briskly to prevent lumps forming. Simmer for 5 minutes. Liquidise soup in a blender or food processor, return to rinsed-out pot and reheat. Add orange juice and zest. Season with salt and pepper. Swirl in the yoghurt, scatter with parsley and serve immediately, piping hot.

Serves 4

SEXY OPTIONS

Fruity Butternut Soup is also delicious served chilled in summer. Chill after liquidising. Stir in the orange juice immediately before serving (do not reheat) and top with finely shredded orange zest and chopped fresh coriander.

COOK'S TIPS

x Save time by buying ready-peeled and cubed butternut.

x You don't need to peel small butternuts: simply cut into chunks, remove seeds and add to soup. The skin softens to a pulp during cooking and adds extra flavour to the soup.

x Adjust the amount of curry powder in this recipe to suit your taste. Remember, however, that curry powder tastes stronger in a soup than it does in a curry or casserole.

x Make a large batch of this soup while butternut is abundant. Freeze it in single portions for quick microwave lunches.

SOUPS

brown onion soup

This easy 'cheat's soup' makes a delicious quick meal.

DRY-FRY MIXTURE
stock made with 875 ml (3½ cups) boiling water and
   15 ml (1 tbsp) Bovril or Marmite

2 large onions, very finely sliced
15 ml (1 tbsp) caster sugar
15 ml (1 tbsp) cornflour
salt and milled black pepper
Giant Crispy Croûtons (see Sexy options), to serve

Dry-fry onions *(see page xi)* in a little of the dry-fry mixture. When onions are soft and browned, add caster sugar and cook for 1 minute, or until onions begin to caramelise. Sprinkle cornflour over onions, stir to coat and cook, stirring, for another minute. Gradually pour in the remaining stock, stirring briskly to prevent lumps forming. Bring to the boil, then reduce heat, cover and simmer for 10 minutes. Season with salt and pepper. Serve hot, and top each portion with a Giant Crispy Croûton.

Serves 3 - 4

SEXY OPTIONS

To make Crispy Croûtons, cut off the crusts of 4 thick slices of wholewheat bread. Cube the bread, then sprinkle lightly with salt water so that cubes are slightly damp but not soggy. Place on a baking sheet and bake at 200°C for about 20 minutes, or until croûtons are crunchy.

To make Garlic Croûtons, spread each slice of bread with a little crushed fresh garlic before baking.

For Giant Crispy Croûtons, use a whole slice of bread for each person and cook for a further 30 minutes.

wholesome chicken soup

Not only is this soup delicious, but it's also economical, 'stretching' two chicken breasts to feed four people.

2 skinned, deboned chicken breasts, very finely chopped
1 onion, chopped
15 ml (1 tbsp) chopped fresh rosemary or 5 ml (1 tsp) dried
5 ml (1 tsp) chopped fresh thyme or 2 ml (½ tsp) dried
2 large potatoes, peeled and cubed
3 ribs celery, trimmed and sliced
1 small bunch fresh parsley, chopped
stock made with 1.37 l (5½ cups) boiling water and 25 ml
   (5 tsp) chicken stock powder
1 bay leaf
250 ml (1 cup) pearl barley
salt and milled black pepper

Dry-fry chicken, onion, rosemary and thyme *(see page xi)*. When chicken is cooked and onion is golden, add potatoes, celery, parsley and 750 ml (3 cups) of the stock. Bring to the boil, then reduce heat, cover and simmer until the potato is tender (about 25 minutes). Liquidise soup in a blender or food processor, return to rinsed-out pot and reheat. Add bay leaf, barley and remaining stock. Cover and simmer for about 1 hour, or until barley is soft yet still slightly chewy. Season with salt and pepper. Remove bay leaf and serve piping hot with crusty bread.

Serves 4

SEXY OPTIONS

For an extra-creamy taste, make up the stock with half fat-free milk and half water. You can also do this with vegetable soups.

Rice or alphabet spaghetti may be used instead of pearl barley. Reduce the total cooking time accordingly.

thai hot prawn soup

A fragrant and exotic soup that never fails to impress dinner party guests.

500 ml (2 cups) water
10 ml (2 tsp) salt
12 raw prawns, shelled
10 ml (2 tsp) cumin seeds
juice of 1 lemon
2 - 3 fresh red or green chillies, de-seeded and finely chopped
5 ml (1 tsp) coconut essence
10 ml (2 tsp) ground ginger
2 cloves garlic, peeled and crushed
45 ml (3 tbsp) caster sugar
5 ml (1 tsp) John West Thai Green Curry paste
stock made with 1 litre (4 cups) boiling water and 20 ml (4 tsp) vegetable or chicken stock powder
125 ml ($1/2$ cup) finely sliced lemon grass (see Cook's Tips)
375 ml ($1^1/2$ cups) mange-touts, topped and tailed
1 packet Shogun Chinese noodles
1 large bunch fresh coriander
250 ml (1 cup) fat-free plain yoghurt
salt and milled black pepper

Put water and 5 ml (1 tsp) of the salt into a large pot and bring to the boil. Put in prawns, wait for the water to begin bubbling vigorously again, then allow prawns to cook for exactly 1 minute. Remove from heat and drain in a colander. Reserve. Put cumin seeds in a dry frying pan and heat until they begin to crackle and release their aromas. Put into a mortar and pestle and grind with the lemon juice and remaining 5 ml (1 tsp) salt to make a thick paste. Reserve. In a large non-stick saucepan, mix together chillies, coconut essence, ginger, garlic, sugar, green curry paste and reserved cumin paste. Cook over a medium heat, stirring constantly with a wooden spoon, until the mixture begins to stick to the bottom of the pan. Add prawns and 60 ml ($1/4$ cup) of the stock and stir briskly. Simmer until most of the liquid has boiled away. Add remaining stock, lemon grass, mange-touts and noodles. Reduce heat and simmer gently for 10 minutes, or until noodles are just cooked.

Just before serving, stir in whole coriander stalks and leaves. Allow soup to stand until coriander wilts. Stir in yoghurt and season with salt and pepper. Serve piping hot.

Serves 4

COOK'S TIPS

x Fresh or frozen prawns can be used in this soup; the cooking time remains the same.

x Use fresh lemon grass stalks if you can find them, but be sure to slice very finely. Use only the lower 10 - 15 cm of the stalk, and discard the fibrous upper part. Bottled lemon grass (John West is a reliable brand) is a very good substitute.

x Try making your own delicious fat-free vegetable stock. Collect vegetable trimmings such as carrot, leek and celery tops, onion rings, parsley stalks, mushroom stalks and so on. Put in a saucepan, cover with cold water and add a bay leaf, a quartered onion, a carrot and a few black peppercorns. If you have fresh parsley or thyme, put those in too. Simmer gently for $1^1/2$ hours. Strain, pressing vegetables down into the strainer with a wooden spoon to extract the juices. Store in a covered container in the fridge or freezer.

x Coconut essence is available from speciality food shops and some home industries outlets. Keep a bottle in the cupboard for delicious fat-free versions of Thai curries.

vichyssoise

This fat-free version of the delicate, creamy soup made from leeks and potatoes is virtually indistinguishable from the cream-rich version.

5 large leeks, white parts only, sliced
3 potatoes, peeled and cubed
stock made with 625 ml (2½ cups) boiling water and 10 ml (2 tsp) chicken stock powder
375 ml (1½ cups) fat-free milk
salt and a pinch of white pepper
freshly grated nutmeg, to taste
snipped chives

Gently dry-fry leeks *(see page xi)* until well softened and golden. Do not allow to brown. Add potatoes, cover with stock and bring to the boil. Reduce heat, cover and simmer until potatoes are tender (about 25 minutes). Skim off any brown froth. Liquidise soup to a fine purée in a blender or food processor and return to rinsed-out pot. Stir in milk (if the soup seems too thick, thin it to the consistency of pouring cream with a little more milk). Reheat gently and allow to simmer for 5 minutes. Season to taste with salt and white pepper. Pour into a glass bowl and chill until very cold (at least 3 hours). Just before serving, stir in a grating of nutmeg, to taste, and sprinkle over the chives.

Serves 4

COOK'S TIPS

x *Be sure to rinse leeks very well before using. Soak the whole leeks in cold water for 10 minutes, then cut a vertical slit most of the way through each leek, fan out the layers and rinse under running water to remove every trace of grit.*

x *Be careful not to add too much white pepper as it has a much more potent bite than milled black pepper. Vichyssoise is supposed to have a very delicate, pale colour, which is why white pepper is used and why the soup is skimmed.*

burnt sherry and mushroom soup

A very thick and rich soup that makes a memorable starter for a winter dinner party.

2 onions, chopped
1 clove garlic, peeled and crushed
30 ml (2 tbsp) soft brown sugar
45 ml (3 tbsp) sherry
2 punnets (about 300 g each) large brown mushrooms, sliced
stock made with 500 ml (2 cups) boiling water and 10 ml (2 tsp) mushroom stock powder
salt and milled black pepper
250 ml (1 cup) fat-free milk
Garlic Croûtons (see Sexy options, page 12), to serve

Dry-fry onions, garlic and sugar *(see page xi)*. Continue cooking over a high heat until the onions are beginning to stick to the pan. Pour in sherry (stand back to avoid being burnt by the steam) and stir briskly to lift residue from bottom of pan. Add mushrooms and dry-fry using some of the mushroom stock. Add remaining stock, cover and simmer for 10 minutes over a medium heat, or until mushrooms are soft and have released their juices. Season with salt and pepper and transfer to a blender or food processor. Add milk and liquidise until very smooth. Return to rinsed-out pot and reheat gently. Season with salt and pepper. Serve hot with Garlic Croûtons.

Serves 4

COOK'S TIPS

x *Burnt Sherry and Mushroom Soup has an unusually thick consistency. If you would prefer a thinner soup, dilute it to the desired consistency with hot chicken stock after liquidising.*

beetroot soup

With its brilliant colour and clean taste, this soup is extremely versatile as it can be served hot or cold.

750 ml (3 cups) peeled, diced beetroot
1 onion, finely chopped
1 leek, trimmed and sliced
1 carrot, peeled and diced
1 turnip, peeled and chopped
1 large potato, peeled and chopped
1 rib celery, trimmed and sliced
20 ml (4 tsp) chicken stock powder
2 bay leaves
30 ml (2 tbsp) chopped fresh parsley
15 ml (1 tbsp) tomato paste
5 ml (1 tsp) caster sugar
15 ml (1 tbsp) lemon juice
1 l (4 cups) water
250 ml (1 cup) fat-free plain yoghurt
salt and milled black pepper

TOPPINGS
$1/2$ English cucumber
finely chopped fresh dill or parsley
finely chopped hard-boiled egg white
fat-free plain yoghurt

Put all ingredients except yoghurt, salt and pepper into a large saucepan and bring to the boil. Reduce heat, cover and simmer until vegetables are very tender (about 1 hour). Remove bay leaves. Liquidise soup in a blender or food processor, return to rinsed-out pot and reheat. Stir in yoghurt. Season with salt and pepper. Serve hot or ice cold, with toppings passed around in separate bowls.

Serves 4

curried mushroom soup

A thick, dark soup with a delicious earthy flavour. Adjust the amount of curry and sherry to suit your personal tastes.

2 onions, sliced or 5 leeks, trimmed and sliced
2 punnets (300 g each) large brown mushrooms, sliced
2 large potatoes, peeled and cubed
stock made with 625 ml ($2^1/2$ cups) boiling water and 10 ml (2 tsp) chicken stock powder
375 ml ($1^1/2$ cups) fat-free milk
5–7.5 ml (1–$1^1/2$ tsp) medium curry powder
1 bay leaf
2 ml ($1/2$ tsp) sugar
45 ml (3 tbsp) sherry
salt and milled black pepper

Dry-fry onions or leeks (see page xi). When onions begin to brown, add mushrooms and potatoes and cook for a further 10 minutes, tossing occasionally and adding a little stock if the vegetables begin to stick. Add stock, milk, curry powder, bay leaf and sugar. Bring to the boil, reduce heat, cover and simmer until potatoes are tender (about 25 minutes). Remove bay leaf. Briefly liquidise soup in a blender or food processor. Return to rinsed-out pot and reheat gently. Season with salt and pepper. Just before serving, stir in sherry. If the soup seems too thick, dilute with a little more milk. Serve piping hot.

Serves 4

COOK'S TIPS

x It's essential to use large brown mushrooms for the Curried Mushroom Soup, as the flavour of button mushrooms is too delicate.

SOUPS

minestrone

This is one of those classic recipes that results in a soup of simple yet seductive flavour and texture. Don't be tempted to add or subtract any ingredients – this fat-free version of the classic vegetable broth will have your friends demanding second or third helpings.

250 ml (1 cup) small white dried beans (see Cook's tips)
1 large onion, thinly sliced or 4 leeks, trimmed and sliced
2 large potatoes, peeled and cubed
3 carrots, peeled and diced
3 ribs celery, trimmed and sliced
2 cloves garlic, peeled and crushed
45 ml (3 tbsp) tomato purée
1 bay leaf
few sprigs fresh parsley
1 sprig fresh thyme or 5 ml (1 tsp) dried thyme
stock made with 1.5 litre (6 cups) boiling water and 45 ml (3 tbsp) vegetable stock powder
6-8 large ripe tomatoes, peeled and chopped or 2 tins (400 g each) chopped, peeled tomatoes plus their juice
500 ml (2 cups) finely shredded cabbage or spinach
250 ml (1 cup) broken-up spaghetti or any small pasta shape
salt and milled black pepper

Soak beans in water overnight or for at least 4 hours. Drain well and reserve. Dry-fry onion *(see page xi)* until softened and golden. Add reserved beans, potatoes, carrots, celery, garlic, tomato purée, bay leaf, parsley and thyme. Cover with stock and bring to the boil. Reduce heat, cover and simmer for 45 - 60 minutes, or until beans are tender and cooked through. Add tomatoes, cabbage or spinach and pasta. Simmer for a further 10 minutes, or until spaghetti is just cooked. Top up with a little more hot stock if necessary. Remove whole herbs, season generously with salt and pepper and serve piping hot.

Serves 6

COOK'S TIPS

x *Any small dried white bean can be used in the minestrone. Small haricot beans and borlotti beans are particularly good. If you're in a hurry, use a tin of white beans, well rinsed and drained, but add them at the end of the cooking time along with the tomatoes and cabbage.*

x *When cooking dried beans, don't add salt until the end of the cooking time, as it toughens the skin of the beans.*

x *If you don't have time to skin the tomatoes, try this trick: Cut each tomato in half. Rest a grater in a shallow soup bowl. Holding half a tomato firmly in the cupped palm of your hand, briskly grate the cut edge on the coarse side of the grater. Continue grating until the skin empties and flattens out in your hand. Discard skin and use pulp in soups or stews.*

SEXY OPTIONS

If you prefer a less chunky vegetable soup, remove the herbs and liquidise the minestrone in batches before adding the pasta.

salads

Salads have changed their attitude! They refuse to be seen as bland meal replacements or 'fillers' any longer! People have always associated salads with dieting. What better way to ruin the reputation of something so special? Apart from the magnificent fibre content, the varied vitamins and minerals their ingredients yield, and the fresh flavours that will whet the appetite of guests at a dinner party, salads are an irreplaceable 'polish' addition to the X Diet, and a wonderful way to 'layer' your food. Like soups, they are not a meal on their own, but delicious and essential side-dishes or starters to energy-filled meals.

If you want to make salads carbohydrate-rich and full of energy, then add beans, pasta or rice, and you'll have quick lunches that travel well to work or school, or braai spreads for guilt-free nibbling as you lazily while the afternoon away.

potato salad

Here is a very basic recipe for fat-free potato salad. You'll never get bored with it — there's an infinite number of interesting variations *(see Sexy options).*

6 waxy potatoes, well scrubbed
1 onion, very finely chopped
125 ml (1/2 cup) chopped fresh parsley
45 ml (3 tbsp) snipped fresh chives

DRESSING
250 ml (1 cup) Knorr Lite Oil-Free Sour Cream and Chives Dressing
125 ml (1/2 cup) fat-free plain yoghurt
60 ml (4 tbsp) fat-free smooth cottage cheese
salt and milled black pepper

Boil potatoes in salted water until just tender (about 20 minutes). Allow to cool for a few minutes, then remove skins and cut potatoes into large cubes. Combine potatoes, onion and parsley in a large bowl. To make dressing, whisk all ingredients until well blended. Pour over potatoes while they are still hot and toss well to combine. Chill for at least 1 hour. Sprinkle with chives just before serving.

Serves 4

COOK'S TIPS

x You don't need to peel the potatoes for the potato salad, in fact the skin adds flavour and texture and contains many vital nutrients. Be sure to scrub the potatoes well before boiling, however.

SEXY OPTIONS

Add a good handful of chopped mint and a generous pinch of ground cumin to the potato salad.

Add 5 ml (1 tsp) crushed garlic and the juice of 1 lemon.

Add 10 ml (2 tsp) creamed horseradish to the dressing and garnish the salad with chopped hard-boiled egg whites. Don't use the yolks — they're packed with fat!

Boiled new potatoes will transform this salad into a taste experience. Simply boil the potatoes in their skins until just tender, cut in half and toss in dressing while still hot. Omit the parsley and chives and add the juice of 1 lemon and a handful of chopped fresh dill.

apple, celery and chickpea salad

Chickpeas add a new twist — and precious carbohydrates — to my fat-free version of the traditional Waldorf Salad.

4 red apples
lemon juice for tossing
8 ribs celery, trimmed and sliced
1 tin (about 400 g) chickpeas, drained
125 ml ($\frac{1}{2}$ cup) seedless raisins

DRESSING
125 ml ($\frac{1}{2}$ cup) Knorr Lite Oil-Free Sour Cream and Chives Dressing
125 ml ($\frac{1}{2}$ cup) fat-free plain yoghurt
30 ml (2 tbsp) fructose or caster sugar
juice of 1 lemon

Core apples but do not peel. Cut into cubes and toss in a little lemon juice to prevent discolouring. Combine apples, celery, chickpeas and raisins in a bowl. To make dressing, whisk together all ingredients until well blended. Pour over salad and toss to combine. Chill for 1 hour before serving.

Serves 4–6

SEXY OPTIONS

Use a combination of red and green apples for extra colour.

Peel two oranges, removing all the pith as well as the skin, and cut across into slices. Reserve the juice. Cut each slice in half and use to garnish the salad. Add the reserved juice to the dressing.

curried rice and peach salad

This substantial salad is ideal for feeding a crowd. Ring the changes by using seasonal fruit (see Sexy options).

1 apple, peeled, cored and coarsely grated
lemon juice for tossing
1 l (4 cups) cooked white rice
2 tins (about 400 g each) peach halves, cubed
125 ml ($\frac{1}{2}$ cup) seedless raisins
1 onion, very finely chopped
1 large green pepper, finely chopped

DRESSING
250 ml (1 cup) Knorr Lite Oil-Free 1000 Islands Dressing
60 ml (4 tbsp) fat-free smooth cottage cheese
45 ml (3 tbsp) fruity chutney
5 ml (1 tsp) mild curry powder
salt and milled black pepper

Toss grated apple in a little lemon juice to prevent discolouring. Tip rice into a large bowl. Add remaining salad ingredients and toss gently to combine. To make dressing, whisk together all ingredients until well blended. Pour over salad and toss to combine. Serve chilled.

Serves 4–6

SEXY OPTIONS

If you decide to use fresh fruit, nectarines, mangoes and apricots are particularly good in this salad. Dried peaches or apricots can be used when fresh fruit is not available. Chop the fruit roughly, then soak in hot rooibos tea for 10 minutes to plump it up.

Create a substantial meal from this rice salad by adding chicken. Thinly slice 3–4 skinned, deboned chicken breasts and dry-fry (see page xi) with a little curry powder. Toss the chicken into the salad before you dress it.

carrot and orange salad

This classic salad has been around for years, but it's a recipe worth reviving as it's totally free of fat and packed with beta-carotene, a vital anti-oxidant. It's a fabulous salad for serving at braais, and kids seem to love it.

1 l (4 cups) coarsely grated carrots
125 ml ($^1/_2$ cup) seedless raisins
4 tinned pineapple rings, cubed
250 ml (1 cup) orange juice
1 bunch watercress

Combine carrots, raisins, pineapple and orange juice in a bowl and toss to combine. Garnish with a ring of watercress sprigs and serve.

Serves 4–6

COOK'S TIPS

x If you can't find watercress, garnish the carrot salad with slices of orange and a modest sprinkling of poppy seeds.

SEXY OPTIONS

Give Carrot and Orange Salad an eastern flavour by stirring 5 ml (1 tsp) each of ground cumin and caster sugar into the orange juice. Garnish with 30 ml (2 tbsp) each chopped fresh mint and chopped fresh coriander.

A handful of snipped chives or spring onions will add a contrasting colour to the salad.

red coleslaw

(See opposite)
This simple but satisfying salad is packed with fibre and vital anti-oxidants.

1 small red cabbage, very finely shredded
375 ml (1$^1/_2$ cups) coarsely grated carrots
250 ml (1 cup) seedless raisins

DRESSING
125 ml ($^1/_2$ cup) Knorr Lite Oil-Free Sour Cream & Chives Dressing
125 ml ($^1/_2$ cup) fat-free plain yoghurt
juice of 1 lemon
10 ml (2 tsp) fructose or caster sugar

Mix cabbage, carrots and raisins in a bowl. To make dressing, whisk together all ingredients until well blended. Pour over salad and toss to combine. Serve chilled.

Serves 4–6

COOK'S TIPS

x Fructose is a natural fruit sugar particularly suited to the X Diet as it has a very low GI (see page ix). It is available from health food shops and large supermarkets.

SEXY OPTIONS

A teaspoon of caraway seeds will add extra flavour to the coleslaw.

Add 15 ml (1 tbsp) French mustard to the dressing for extra zip.

Tart apples, such as Granny Smiths, add a sweet note to coleslaw. Remember to toss the slices in lemon juice to prevent them from discolouring.

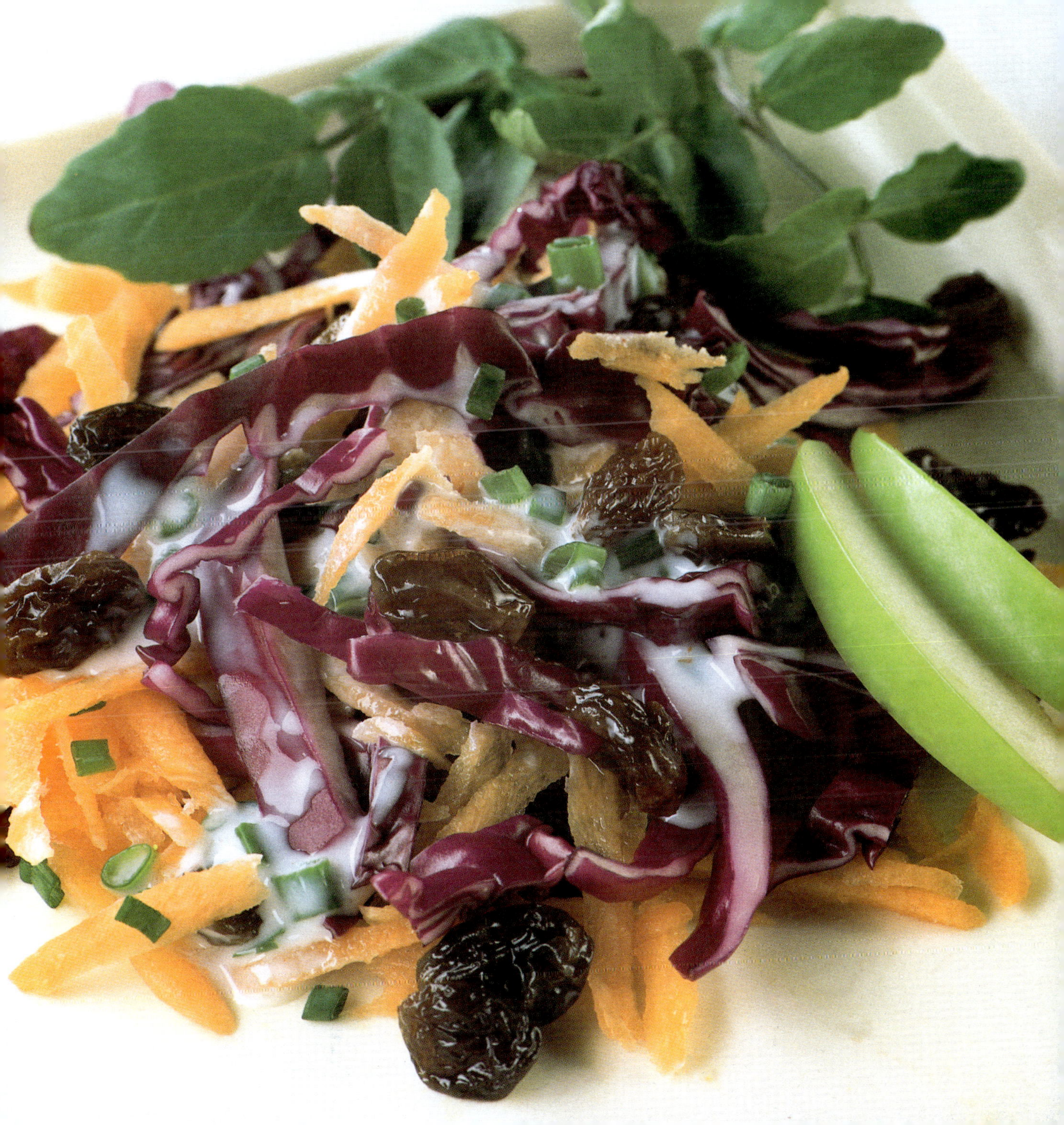

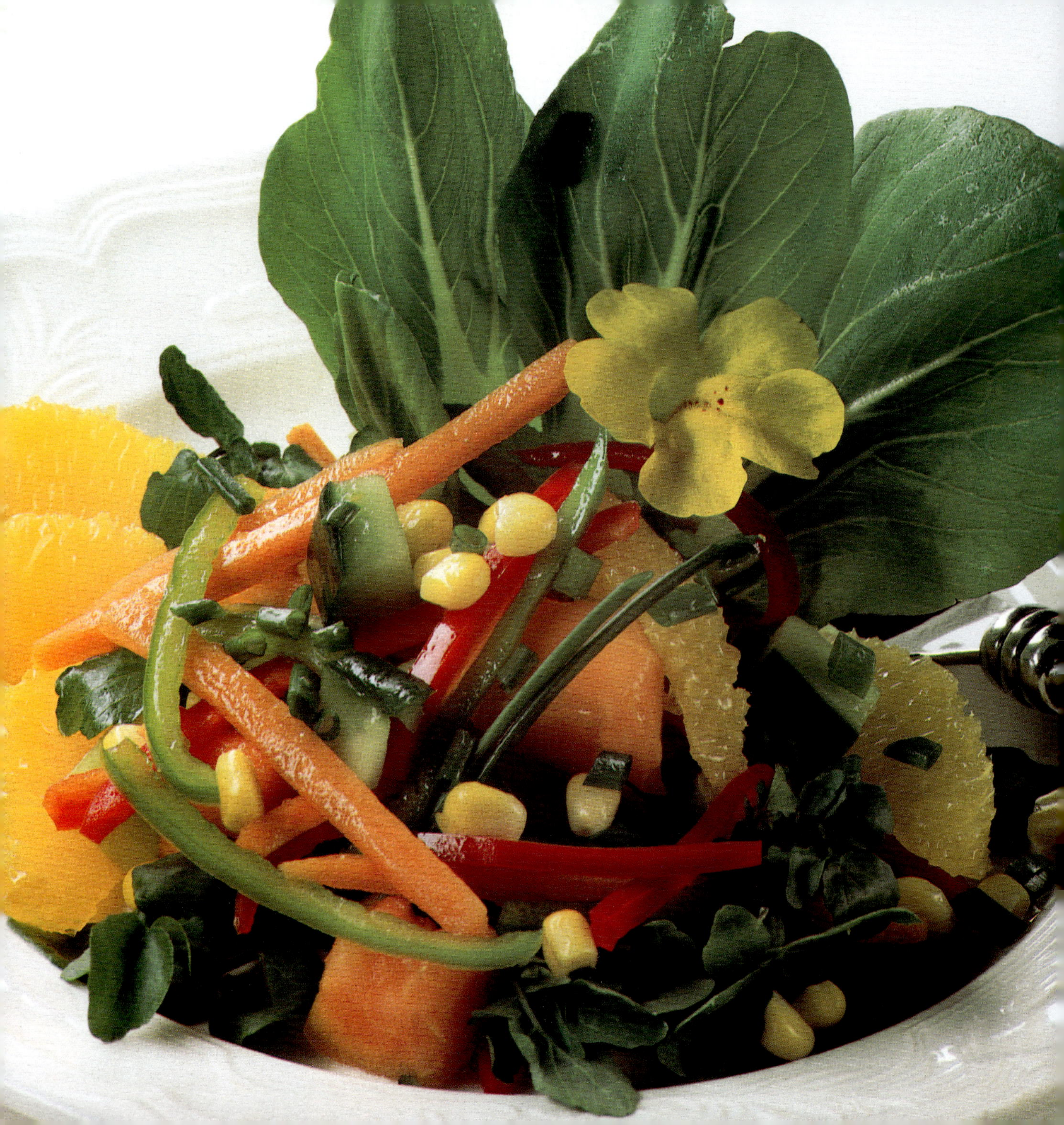

summer salad

(See opposite)

My guests always exclaim over this light and colourful summer salad, with its unusual flower garnish. The watercress and rocket belong to the group of dark green and leafy special vegetables, so eat up!

3 oranges
1 'pillow' packet fresh rocket or young spinach
1 'pillow' packet watercress
1 red pepper, very finely sliced
1 green pepper, very finely sliced
1 ripe papino, peeled, de-seeded and cubed
6 spring onions, finely sliced
1 cucumber, cubed
6 carrots, peeled and cut into thin matchsticks
1 tin (about 400 g) whole kernel sweetcorn, drained
8 nasturtium flowers and 8 leaves

DRESSING
80 ml (1/3 cup) raspberry vinegar
80 ml (1/3 cup) orange juice
45 ml (3 tbsp) runny honey, warmed (see Cook's tips, page 23)

Peel oranges over a bowl and cut out segments *(see Cook's tips)*. Reserve juice. Wash rocket or spinach and watercress and pat or spin dry. Arrange rocket and watercress in a large bowl. Scatter over red pepper, green pepper, papino, spring onions, cucumber, carrots and sweetcorn. To make dressing, combine all ingredients in a screw-top jar and shake until well blended. Pour over salad and toss well to combine. Garnish with nasturtium flowers and leaves and serve.

Serves 4–6

COOK'S TIPS

x To segment an orange neatly, first peel the orange as you would an apple, using a sharp knife and taking care to remove every trace of white pith. Hold the orange over a bowl to catch the juice. Cut on either side of the membranes that divide the segments, making sure you cut all the way to the centre. Gently twist the knife to release the segment, leaving the membrane behind. Repeat until you have removed all the segments.

x If you're short of time, replace the oranges with well-drained tinned mandarins. Tinned litchis also work well in this salad.

SEXY OPTIONS

If you can't find nasturtium flowers, use any other edible flower, such as chive flowers, borage flowers or violets.

Transform this salad into a satisfying meal by adding potatoes. Boil 12 new potatoes in their skins, drain well, cut in half and add to the salad immediately before serving. The contrast of hot potato and cool crunchy salad is spectacular.

Add a tin of drained asparagus tips, or use steamed fresh asparagus when it's in season.

couscous salad

Once you taste this delicious and substantial salad, you'll wonder how you ever entertained without it.

1 packet (500 g) pre-cooked couscous
stock made with 750 ml (3 cups) boiling water and 20 ml
  (4 tsp) chicken stock powder
250 ml (1 cup) seedless raisins or sultanas
2 bunches spring onions, finely chopped
6–8 baby marrows, finely sliced
60 ml (4 tbsp) fresh basil leaves, torn into pieces
60 ml (4 tbsp) finely chopped fresh parsley
60 ml (4 tbsp) finely chopped fresh mint

DRESSING
125 ml ($^1/_2$ cup) lemon juice
finely grated zest of 1 orange
125 ml ($^1/_2$ cup) orange juice
30 ml (2 tbsp) runny honey, warmed (see Cook's tips, page 23)
7 ml (1 heaped tsp) paprika
10 ml (2 tsp) salt
milled black pepper

Prepare couscous as directed on packet, using the stock as cooking liquid. Tip into a large bowl. Add raisins, spring onions, baby marrows, basil, parsley and mint and toss gently to combine. To make dressing, combine all ingredients in a screw-top jar and shake until well blended. Pour over salad and toss well to combine. Serve warm or at room temperature.

Serves 4

COOK'S TIPS

x If the couscous is still warm when you add the other ingredients and the dressing, it will soak up more of the flavours.

SEXY OPTIONS

In place of raisins, use dried apricots. Soak 250 ml (1 cup) dried apricots in orange juice or rooibos tea for 20 minutes. Drain and roughly chop.

marinated tomatoes

A simple dish with a knock-out taste. For best results, make the salad the night before.

6 firm, ripe tomatoes, finely sliced
2 onions, finely sliced
125 ml ($^1/_2$ cup) balsamic vinegar
5 ml (1 tsp) salt
60 ml (4 tbsp) soft brown sugar
milled black pepper
1 bunch fresh chives, finely snipped

Layer tomato and onion slices in a flat ceramic dish. Combine vinegar, salt and sugar in a saucepan and heat gently, stirring constantly, until sugar has dissolved. Alternatively, put in a jug and microwave on high for about 1 minute, stirring once or twice. Pour hot dressing over tomatoes and onions. Cover dish with clingwrap and leave to stand at room temperature overnight, or for at least 6 hours, turning occasionally if possible. Just before serving, grind plenty of black pepper over dish and sprinkle generously with chives. Serve with a coarse-textured bread, such as Italian bread, to mop up the juices.

Serves 4–6

SEXY OPTIONS

Thinly slice a block of fat-free Philadelphia cream cheese and arrange on top of the salad immediately before serving.

tuna pasta salad

Another basic recipe that can be adapted according to your taste and what's in season. Try it with poached and flaked fresh line fish, cooked prawns or calamari rings.

500 ml (2 cups) frozen peas
1 l (4 cups) cooked pasta shapes
5 ml (1 tsp) cayenne pepper, or to taste
1 tin (200 g) tuna in brine, drained and flaked
1 onion, finely chopped
1 red pepper, finely chopped
1 green or yellow pepper, finely chopped
2 ripe tomatoes, chopped
4 spring onions, finely sliced

DRESSING
250 ml (1 cup) Knorr Lite Oil-Free 1000 Islands Dressing
125 ml (1/2 cup) fat-free plain yoghurt
125 ml (1/2 cup) fat-free smooth cottage cheese
salt and milled black pepper

Cook peas as directed on the packet and drain well. In a large bowl, combine peas, pasta, cayenne pepper, tuna, onion, peppers and tomatoes. Toss well to combine. To make dressing, whisk together all ingredients until well blended. Pour over salad and toss to combine. Scatter with spring onions and serve chilled.

Serves 4–6

COOK'S TIPS

x Use roast peppers in this salad for extra flavour. Place whole peppers under a blazing hot grill and cook until skin begins to blacken and blister. Place in a paper bag for 10 minutes to cool. Rub off the blackened skin (it's easier to do this under running water) and slice finely.

rice, pineapple and sprout salad

A simple salad with an unexpected crunch. Be sure to use basmati rice, which has an unusual flavour essential to the success of the dish.

1 l (4 cups) cooked, cooled basmati rice
500 ml (2 cups) mung-bean or alfalfa sprouts
1 bunch spring onions, finely sliced
500 ml (2 cups) finely chopped fresh pineapple
1 tin (400 g) water chestnuts, drained and finely sliced

DRESSING
250 ml (1 cup) soy sauce
125 ml (1/2 cup) freshly squeezed orange juice
30 ml (2 tbsp) runny honey, warmed (see Cook's tips)
salt and milled black pepper

Combine salad ingredients in a bowl. To make dressing, combine soy sauce, orange juice and honey in a screw-top jar and shake well to combine. Season to taste with salt and pepper. Pour over salad and toss well to combine. Serve immediately.

Serves 6

COOK'S TIPS

x Warming honey makes it more liquid and easier to work with. Stand the jar in a saucepan of hot water for a few minutes, until the honey softens. Before removing it from the jar, also warm the spoon, and you'll find the honey slides off easily.

prawn salad with hot orange dressing

With its exotic hot ginger and orange dressing, this salad makes a stunning starter for a dinner party.

2 ripe papinos
1 butter lettuce
½ English cucumber, finely sliced
1 onion, very finely sliced

DRESSING
16 small, raw, shelled prawns
10 ml (2 tsp) ground ginger
2 cloves garlic, peeled and crushed
juice of 5 oranges
1 small bunch fresh coriander, finely chopped
salt and milled black pepper

Peel and de-seed papinos and cut lengthways into thin strips. Rinse lettuce and pat or spin dry. Divide lettuce leaves between four serving plates and arrange cucumber slices on top in an overlapping ring. Scatter onion rings over cucumber. Arrange sliced papino on top. To make dressing, heat a non-stick frying pan. Quickly dry-fry prawns, ginger and garlic (see page xi), using orange juice to moisten, until prawns are pink and firm (about 5 minutes). Add remaining orange juice and coriander, stir briskly to deglaze pan, reduce heat and allow to bubble softly for a further 2 minutes. Season with salt and pepper. Spoon hot prawn dressing over salads and serve immediately.

Serves 4

SEXY OPTIONS

Fresh asparagus tips, steamed until tender, add a note of luxury to this salad.

For an Oriental note, use 5 ml (1 tsp) grated fresh ginger in place of ground ginger and 5 ml (1 tsp) Thai fish sauce.

curried three-bean salad

A spicy version of an old family favourite. This recipe contains a very unusual ingredient — Coca-Cola — which adds that indefinable 'something' to the salad. Serve with chunky pieces of bread for mopping up the juices.

1 tin (400 g) butter beans, rinsed and drained
1 tin (400 g) kidney beans, rinsed and drained
1 tin (400 g) chickpeas, rinsed and drained
salt and milled black pepper

DRESSING
1 onion, finely sliced
1 green pepper, finely sliced
5 ml (1 tsp) ground cumin
5 ml (1 tsp) mild curry powder
2 ml (½ tsp) turmeric
250 ml (1 cup) Coca-Cola
125 ml (½ cup) balsamic vinegar

Put beans into a large bowl and toss to combine. To make dressing, dry-fry onion and green pepper (see page xi). When onion is soft, add cumin, curry powder and turmeric and stir well to coat. Toss over a high heat until all liquid has evaporated and spices are beginning to stick to the pan. Add a few tablespoons of Coca-Cola and continue to cook, tossing briskly. When the pan is dry again and the spices smell aromatic, add remaining cola. Allow to bubble and reduce for a few more minutes. Remove pan from heat and stir in vinegar. Pour hot dressing over beans and mix well to combine. Season with salt and milled black pepper. Leave to cool then chill overnight before serving.

Serves 6

COOK'S TIPS

* Any cooked pulse, including cooked or tinned lentils, can be used in this salad. You can even use baked beans, but first rinse them in a sieve to wash off the tomato sauce.

vegetables

*E*verybody knows that vegetables are an integral part of any healthy eating plan. But they are perhaps more important to the X Diet than to most eating plans, because they should be eaten in enormous quantities, and I mean enormous! Although they don't provide much in the way of energy, vegetables do give us the fundamental vitamins and minerals needed for proper metabolic function. Research has proved beyond doubt that they can protect you from the serious degenerative diseases that plague our modern lifestyles, including cancer and heart disease. There is no simple substitute for them — not even the most expensive vitamin tablets will do!

Because many people regard vegetables as a staple of any fat-reducing regime, they tend to cook and serve them in a tasteless (and frankly boring) way — steamed and sprinkled with lemon juice, boiled and dredged with herb salt, or just plain raw without even the pleasure of a dipping sauce. Now is the time to abandon these humdrum recipes and to start to savour the exciting flavours offered by these nutritional marvels!

A particularly important facet of the X Diet is that it's vital to ensure a daily ration of the 'Special Seven' vegetables (*see page ix*). These are, in no particular order, broccoli, spinach, butternut, pumpkin, carrots, red cabbage and beetroot, all of which are spectacularly rich in beta-carotene, a vital anti-oxidant. But eating your required two cups a day is not always as easy as it sounds, particularly if you're on the run all day and don't have time to peel carrots or chop beetroot. For this reason, you will find many convenient and quick recipes in this chapter containing the Special Seven in one form or another. Try them out on your children, chances are they'll become life-long devotees.

side dishes

creamed spinach

This dish often becomes a mainstay of the X Diet for my patients, who appreciate its 'creamy' texture. Spinach is one of the special vegetables, so allow one cup per person, please!

2 large bunches spinach
80 ml (1/3 cup) fat-free milk powder
60 ml (1/4 cup) cornflour
500 ml (2 cups) fat-free milk
10 ml (2 tsp) vegetable stock powder
30 ml (2 tbsp) sherry
30 ml (2 tbsp) sugar
2 cloves garlic, peeled and crushed, or to taste
salt and milled black pepper

Pull stalks and any tough strands off spinach leaves and rinse well to remove all traces of grit. Place wet spinach in a large pot over a medium heat. Cover and cook, stirring regularly, for 10–15 minutes, or until leaves are well wilted. While spinach is cooking, make white sauce. Put milk powder and cornflour into a teacup and add enough of the milk to mix to a smooth, runny paste. Heat remaining milk in a saucepan. When milk is very hot (but not boiling), whisk in cornflour paste. Continue to cook over a low heat, stirring constantly, until sauce is thick and smooth. Stir in stock powder, sherry, sugar and garlic. Season generously with salt and pepper. Put cooked spinach in a colander and press down with a small plate to extract as much water as possible. Tip onto a chopping board and chop roughly. Stir spinach into sauce and serve very hot.

Serves 3–4

COOK'S TIPS

x *If the spinach seems very wet after draining, return it to the cooking pot for a few minutes and allow it to dry over the heat.*

x *What we call 'spinach' in South Africa is actually Swiss chard. If you can find real spinach, use that by all means, but remember that it may take slightly less time to cook.*

SEXY OPTIONS

Add a generous pinch of freshly grated nutmeg to the white sauce.

Dry-fry *(see page xi)* 1 punnet (about 300 g) of sliced button mushrooms, using a little white wine to moisten. Stir into the white sauce along with the cooked spinach.

spicy mashed butternut

Butternut is one of those special vegetables that tastes wonderful all on its own. This recipe takes a little time, but is one of my favourite ways of cooking butternut.

750 ml (3 cups) hot, cooked butternut (see Cook's tips)
125 ml (1/2 cup) buttermilk
45 ml (3 tbsp) soft brown sugar
5 ml (1 tsp) cinnamon
salt and milled black pepper

Preheat oven to 180 °C. Put hot butternut in a deep bowl. Mash to a purée with a potato masher, adding just enough buttermilk to make a smooth, soft paste. Beat in sugar and cinnamon and season to taste with salt and pepper. Tip into a non-stick ovenproof dish, cover with tin foil and put in the oven for about 15 minutes, to reheat gently. Serve hot.

Serves 4

SEXY OPTIONS

Add the finely grated zest of half an orange and a pinch of ground coriander to mashed or baked butternut.

Combine mashed butternut with an equal quantity of mashed potato or sweet potato. If the mixture seems too stiff, moisten with a little more buttermilk. Tip into a casserole dish, fluff up top with a fork and bake at 180°C for 10 minutes, or until very hot.

COOK'S TIPS

x *To cook butternut, cut in half lengthways, remove seeds and chop into large chunks. Don't bother to peel the butternut — the skins will cook to a soft pulp. Cover with a stock made of boiling water and vegetable stock powder. Simmer butternut gently for about 30 minutes, or until it is quite tender, then drain well.*

butternut on the braai

A simple but moreish way of cooking butternut on the braai. Serve this to your vegetarian friends and they won't complain about braais again!

1 large butternut
1 tomato, chopped
1 green pepper, chopped
250 ml (1 cup) fruity chutney
1 onion, thinly sliced
salt and milled black pepper

Cut butternut in half lengthways and scoop out seeds with a metal spoon. Mix together tomato and green pepper and stuff into hollows. Spread chutney over the entire cut surfaces of both halves, then sprinkle onion rings on top. Season with salt and pepper. Carefully reassemble butternut by pressing the two halves back together. Place on a large double piece of tin foil, shiny side up, and wrap tightly to make a secure parcel. Place butternut in the hot coals of the fire and cook, turning frequently, for 1–1 1/2 hours. The butternut is cooked when a sharp knife easily pierces the flesh. Unwrap butternut and cut crossways into thick slices. Serve hot.

Serves 4

curried chickpeas

A fragrant dish of energy-packed chickpeas simmered with spices and tomatoes. Serve it as a side dish with fish or chicken, or as a main course with basmati rice.

2 large onions, chopped
3 cloves garlic, peeled and crushed
1 fresh red or green chilli, de-seeded and finely chopped
30 ml (2 tbsp) grated fresh ginger
5 ml (1 tsp) ground coriander
5 ml (1 tsp) cumin seeds
5 ml (1 tsp) turmeric
60 ml (1/4 cup) Coca-Cola
2 tins (about 400 g each) chickpeas, rinsed and drained
1 tin (400 g) chopped, peeled tomatoes
5 ml (1 tsp) brown sugar
salt and milled black pepper
5 ml (1 tsp) garam masala

Dry-fry onions, garlic, chilli, ginger, coriander, cumin and turmeric, using the cola to moisten (*see page xi*). When the onions are soft and golden and the spices smell fragrant, add chickpeas, tomatoes and brown sugar. Reduce heat and simmer very gently for about 30 minutes, stirring frequently. Season with salt and pepper. Stir in garam masala and serve immediately.

Serves 4–6

SEXY OPTIONS

Top each portion with a dollop of fat-free plain yoghurt and a scattering of chopped fresh coriander.

Add a few whole cardamom pods, four whole cloves and two cinnamon sticks to the chickpeas for extra fragrance. Remove before serving.

parsnip purée

An unusual dish delicately flavoured with orange. You can vary the basic recipe by adding whisked egg whites and allowing the dish to puff up in the oven (*see Sexy options*).

6 large parsnips (about 1 kg)
60 ml (1/4 cup) buttermilk
finely grated zest and juice of 1 orange
juice of 1 lemon
salt and milled black pepper
chopped fresh parsley

Peel parsnips and cut into chunks. Cook in boiling salted water until quite tender. Drain well. Put into a food processor or blender, add buttermilk and process to a purée. Add orange zest and juice and lemon juice. Season to taste with salt and pepper. Tip into a warmed bowl, smooth the top, sprinkle with parsley and serve hot.

Serves 4

SEXY OPTIONS

Make a Parsnip Puff using this purée. Preheat the oven to 180°C. After you have puréed and seasoned the parsnips, fold in the stiffly beaten whites of 2 small eggs. Tip the mixture into a non-stick ovenproof dish, top with Kellogg's Cornflakes Crumbs and bake for 30 minutes, or until puffed and golden.

For a more substantial dish, use half potatoes and half parsnips to make the purée. Top with a generous grating of nutmeg and plenty of black pepper.

carrots in yoghurt

An interesting way to serve carrots. Serve hot as a side dish or cold as a sambal with curry.

500 ml (2 cups) fresh young carrots or frozen sliced carrots
5 ml (1 tsp) sugar
5 ml (1 tsp) ground cumin
juice of ½ lemon
250 ml (1 cup) fat-free plain yoghurt
salt and milled black pepper
fresh coriander sprigs

If using fresh carrots, peel and slice. Put carrots and sugar in a saucepan, add enough water to cover and boil until just tender. Drain well and arrange in a warmed vegetable dish. In a jug, combine cumin, lemon juice and yoghurt. Season to taste with salt and pepper. Pour over hot carrots. Garnish with a few sprigs of fresh coriander and serve.

Serves 4

oven-baked crisps

These fat-free crisps are a good alternative to bowls of greasy peanuts. Children are particularly fond of them, so make a lot!

4 large potatoes
125 ml (½ cup) tomato sauce
salt
vinegar for serving

Preheat oven to 220 °C. Slice potatoes into very thin discs. Dip each slice into tomato sauce, then lay it flat on a non-stick baking tray. Sprinkle with a little salt and bake for about 25 minutes, until the slices begin to curl. Turn them over using tongs or a spatula and sprinkle with a little more salt. Bake for a further 20–25 minutes until the slices are crispy. Serve hot sprinkled with vinegar and with more tomato sauce for dipping.

Serves 4

SEXY OPTIONS

Dip the slices in a mixture of chutney and vinegar instead of tomato sauce.

Sprinkle with seasoned sea salt and a pinch of cayenne pepper for an extra-spicy snack.

roast potatoes

These look and taste virtually the same as traditional roast potatoes, but don't contain any fat.

4 large potatoes, peeled
60 ml (¼ cup) chicken stock powder
5 ml (1 tsp) salt

Preheat oven to 200 °C. Cut the potatoes into equal-sized chunks. Put potatoes in a pot and add enough boiling water to cover. Add stock powder and salt, bring to the boil and parboil potatoes for about 10–15 minutes. Drain well. Place potatoes on a non-stick baking tray and bake until golden and crisp (about 30 minutes). Serve hot with plenty of fat-free gravy (see page 90).

Serves 4

SEXY OPTIONS

To make sticky potatoes, brush each parboiled potato chunk generously with fruity chutney before baking.

For extra-crunchy potatoes, return the parboiled potatoes to the pan after you have drained them and shake for a few minutes over the heat so that the surface roughens and dries out. Or use a fork to scratch grooves into the surface of each one. Then bake in the normal way.

golden potato wedges

Resembling chunky, crispy chips, these wedges are prepared in a jiffy and make wonderful hot snacks.

4 large potatoes
45 ml (3 tbsp) chicken spice
5 ml (1 tsp) turmeric
salt and milled black pepper

Preheat oven to 200 °C. Scrub potatoes but do not peel. Cut each potato in half lengthways, then cut each half into 3 equal wedges. Place wedges, cut sides facing up, on a non-stick baking tray. Sprinkle with chicken spice and turmeric and season to taste with salt and pepper. Bake for 30–40 minutes, or until puffed and golden.

Serves 4

COOK'S TIPS

x Instead of turmeric, use a little paprika and a sprinkling of vegetable stock powder.

crispy potato croquettes

An elegant way to serve potatoes. If you don't like crumbed potatoes, try making Duchesse Potatoes *(see Sexy options)*.

4 large, floury potatoes, peeled and cubed
125 ml ($^1/_2$ cup) buttermilk
salt and white pepper
3 egg whites, lightly beaten
250–500 ml (1–2 cups) Kellogg's Cornflakes Crumbs

Preheat oven to 180 °C. Cook potatoes in plenty of boiling, salted water until tender (about 25 minutes). Drain well and return to pot. If potatoes are still a little wet, toss over a medium heat for a few minutes to dry out. Using a potato masher, mash well, adding just enough of the buttermilk to result in a smooth paste that can hold its shape. Remove from heat and allow to cool. If the mixture seems lumpy, push through a sieve. Season to taste with salt and pepper. Take a heaped tablespoon of mash, roll into a ball between floured palms and dip in egg white. Roll in crumbs to coat completely, then place on a non-stick baking tray. Repeat until you have used up all the mash. Bake for about 15 minutes, or until coating is golden and crispy. Serve hot.

Serves 4–6

SEXY OPTIONS

Adding 2 ml ($^1/_2$ tsp) baking powder to the mash will make extra light and fluffy potato croquettes.

To make Duchesse Potatoes, add 5 ml (1 tsp) baking powder and a little more buttermilk to loosen the mixture. Place in a piping bag fitted with a large star nozzle and pipe rosettes of potato onto a non-stick baking sheet. Bake at 180 °C for 10–15 minutes, or until golden and puffed. Lift off with a spatula. Serve with fish or chicken.

potato and mushroom bake

A fat-free version of classic scalloped potatoes. This dish is particularly good served with fish.

6 large potatoes
1 punnet (about 300 g) button mushrooms
1 large onion, finely sliced
1 l (4 cups) fat-free milk
60 ml (¼ cup) fat-free milk powder
4–6 cloves garlic, peeled and crushed, to taste
5 ml (1 tsp) prepared English mustard
10 ml (2 tsp) cayenne pepper, or to taste
10 ml (2 tsp) Cubbs Bacon and Onion Party Dip powder (see Cook's tips)

Preheat oven to 180 °C. Scrub potatoes very well but do not peel. Slice into very thin discs. Wipe mushrooms and slice finely. Separate onion slices into rings. In a bowl, combine milk, milk powder, garlic, mustard and cayenne pepper to taste. Whisk in dip powder. Put a quarter of the potato slices in a shallow, non-stick ovenproof dish. Top with a third of the mushroom slices and a third of the onion rings. Pour in enough of the milk mixture just to submerge the layer. Add another layer of potatoes, mushrooms and onions and top up with milk. Continue until all the mushrooms and onions are used up, finishing with a layer of potato slices. Bake until potatoes are very tender (about 1 hour). Serve hot.

Serves 4–6

COOK'S TIPS

x If you can't find Cubbs Party Dip, use 30 ml (2 tbsp) onion soup powder instead. Be sure to check, however, that it contains less than 3 g fat per 100 g. Chicken or mushroom stock powder may also be used in place of the dip powder.

SEXY OPTIONS

Five minutes before the end of cooking time, sprinkle the potato bake with a handful of Kellogg's Cornflakes Crumbs and some paprika. Place under a preheated grill and cook for 5 minutes, or until topping is golden.

'cheesy' stuffed potatoes

This recipe contains not a crumb of cheese, which is forbidden on the X Diet. But who needs cheese when potatoes taste this good? Serve at braais, or as an accompaniment to grilled chicken kebabs or chicken burgers.

4 large potatoes
125 ml (½ cup) buttermilk
1 small bunch spring onions, very finely chopped
5 ml (1 tsp) cayenne pepper
5 ml (1 tsp) prepared English mustard
10 ml (2 tsp) soft brown sugar
5 ml (1 tsp) salt
milled black pepper
fat-free milk

Preheat oven to 200 °C. Scrub potatoes well but do not peel. Rub each wet potato with salt and cut a slit in each one. Place on a baking tray and bake until tender (1–1½ hours). Allow potatoes to cool slightly, then cut each one in half. Carefully scoop out potato flesh, leaving a 2 mm shell of skin and flesh. In a bowl, combine potato flesh, buttermilk, spring onions, cayenne pepper, mustard, sugar, salt and pepper. Mash to a smooth purée with a potato masher, adding enough fat-free milk to make a soft (but not sloppy) mixture. Pile mixture back into potato skins, heaping up the filling so that the top is rounded. Sprinkle with a little extra cayenne pepper. Put potatoes on a baking sheet and bake for a further 10–15 minutes, or until topping is golden and crisp.

Serves 4

broccoli gratin

This is a good way to get children to eat broccoli if they're not keen on the idea — and eat broccoli they should, as it's one of the cancer-fighting superstars of the vegetable world.

1 large head fresh broccoli or 4 cups frozen broccoli
60 ml (¼ cup) cornflour
1 l (4 cups) fat-free milk
1 sachet (15 g) Cubbs Bacon and Onion Party Dip powder
   (see Cook's tips, page 31)
10 ml (2 tsp) prepared English mustard
5 ml (1 tsp) cayenne pepper, or to taste
10 ml (2 tsp) sugar
5 ml (1 tsp) salt
milled black pepper
1 onion, finely sliced

Preheat oven to 180 °C. Rinse broccoli and break into florets the size of golf balls. Cook in plenty of boiling salted water until just tender (about 10 minutes). Drain. Arrange broccoli in a single layer in a shallow non-stick ovenproof dish. Put cornflour in a teacup and add just enough of the milk to make a smooth, runny paste. Heat remaining milk in a saucepan and stir in dip powder. When milk is very hot (but not boiling), whisk in cornflour paste. Cook over a low heat, stirring constantly, until sauce is thick and smooth. Stir in mustard, cayenne pepper and sugar. Season with salt and pepper. Pour sauce over broccoli. Sprinkle with onion rings and a little more cayenne pepper. Bake for 30 minutes, or until golden brown. Serve hot.

Serves 4

SEXY OPTIONS

Soy sauce goes particularly well with broccoli. Omit the mustard and add 30 ml (2 tbsp) dark soy sauce to the white sauce.

braised fennel with tomato

(See opposite)

An easy way of cooking a very aristocratic vegetable. Baked fennel is smart enough for the most elegant of dinner parties and is particularly good with fish. When fennel is not in season, use leeks instead.

3 fennel bulbs
6 tomatoes
3 cloves garlic, peeled and crushed
5 ml (1 tsp) finely grated lemon zest
1 large onion, very finely chopped
stock made with 185 ml (¾ cup) boiling water and 5 ml
   (1 tsp) vegetable stock
salt and milled black pepper
chopped fresh parsley

Preheat oven to 180 °C. Trim and wash fennel bulbs well, cut off any brown spots and cut into quarters. Cut any tough inner core from each quarter. Cook in plenty of boiling salted water for 15 minutes, or until just tender. Drain well in a colander and arrange in a single layer in a shallow ovenproof dish. Dip tomatoes in boiling water for 60 seconds, then slip off skins and cut into quarters. Scatter tomatoes, garlic, lemon zest and onion over fennel and cover with hot stock. Mix gently to combine. Season with salt and pepper. Cover with tin foil and bake for 1 hour, or until very tender. Just before serving, grind over more black pepper and scatter with chopped fresh parsley. Serve hot, or cold the next day.

Serves 4

SEXY OPTIONS

Scatter a handful of Kellogg's Cornflakes Crumbs and a little more finely grated lemon zest over the fennel 10 minutes before the end of the cooking time. Return to the oven and cook until crumb topping is golden and crisp.

VEGETABLES

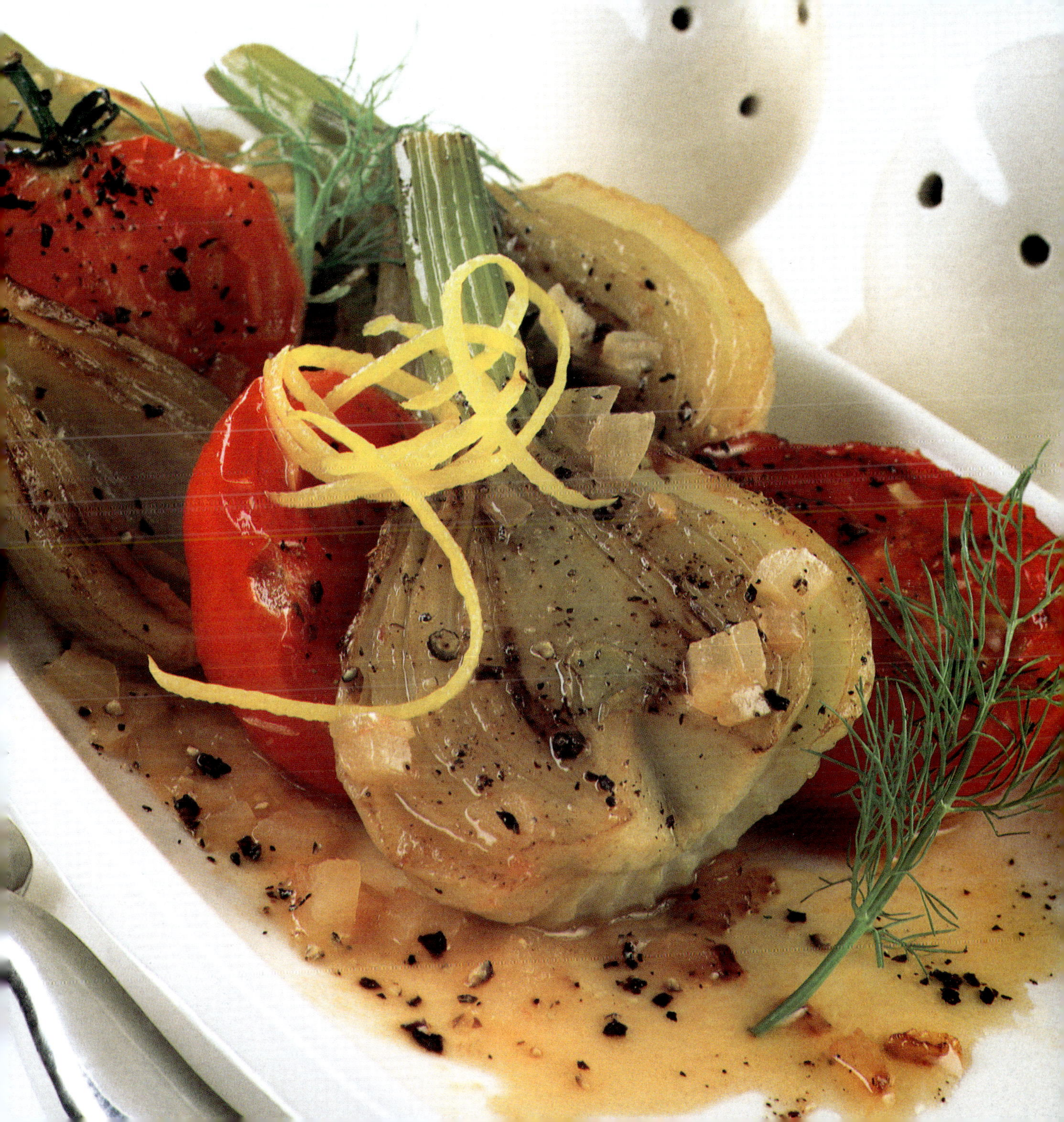

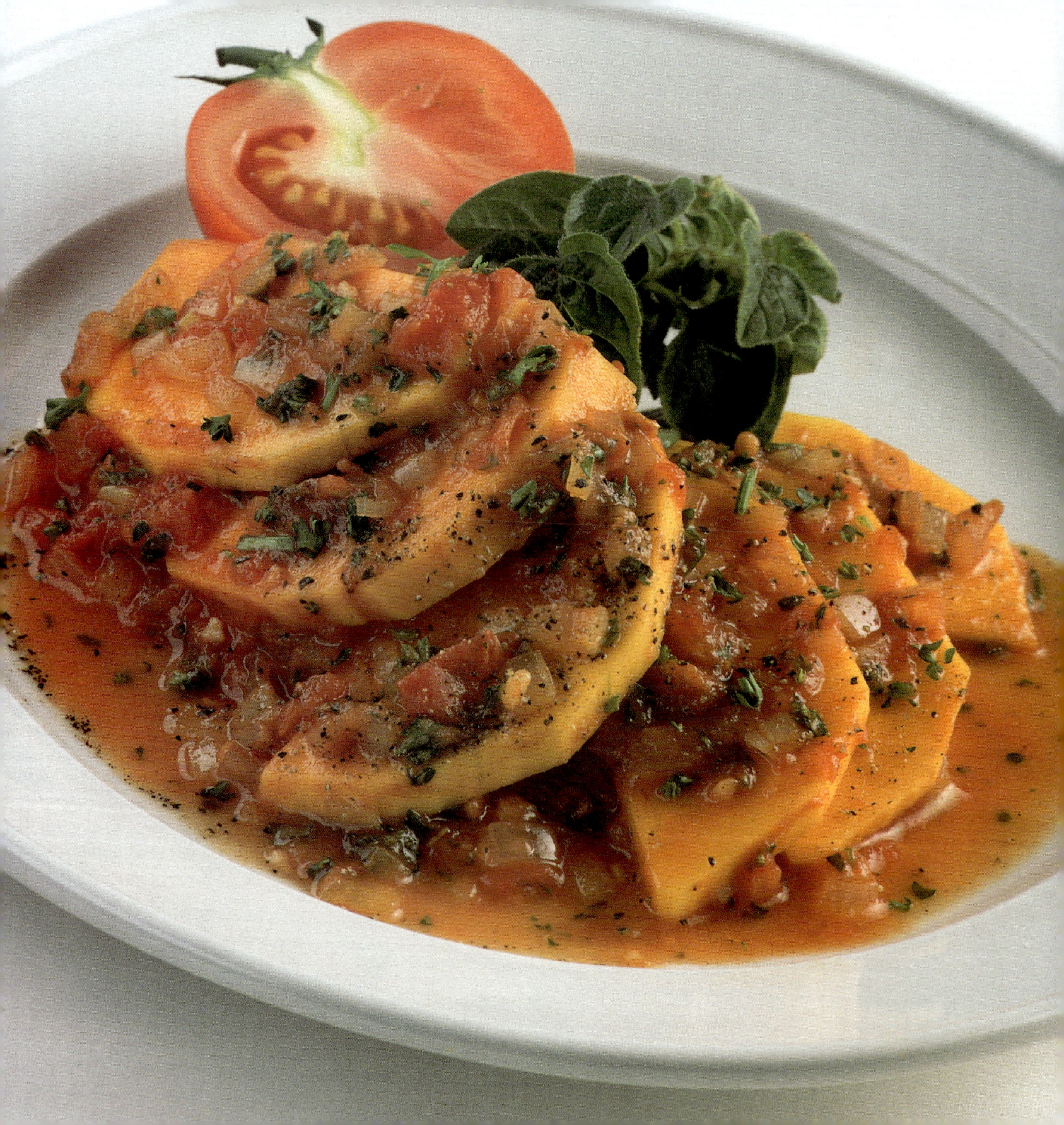

greek-style butternut

(See opposite)
This homely vegetable dish is ideal for cold winter nights and is very economical for feeding a crowd. Serve it with plenty of hot crusty bread.

2 onions, chopped
1 tin (400 g) chopped, peeled tomatoes
3 cloves garlic, peeled and crushed
5 ml (1 tsp) cinnamon, or to taste
15 ml (1 tbsp) chopped fresh oregano or 5 ml (1 tsp) dried oregano
125 ml ($^1/_2$ cup) chopped fresh parsley
10 ml (2 tsp) runny honey (see Cook's tips, page 23)
1 l (4 cups) peeled, sliced or diced butternut
salt and milled black pepper

Dry-fry onions in a large saucepan (*see page xi*). When onions are soft and golden, add tomatoes, garlic, cinnamon, oregano, parsley, honey and butternut. Season with salt and pepper. Simmer, stirring occasionally, until butternut is tender, adding a little water if necessary. Serve hot.

Serves 4–6

COOK'S TIPS

x Use left-over Greek-Style Butternut to make a quick lunch soup. Tip into the goblet of a liquidiser, add a cup or two of hot stock and whizz to a fine purée.

grilled mushrooms

Large brown mushrooms have a deliciously 'meaty' texture and flavour. This very garlicky dish is ideal for vegetarians.

2 punnets (about 300 g each) large brown mushrooms
8–10 cloves garlic, peeled and very finely chopped
60 ml ($^1/_4$ cup) chopped fresh parsley
60 ml ($^1/_4$ cup) boiling water
2 ml ($^1/_2$ tsp) stock powder
2 green or red peppers, finely sliced into rings
milled sea salt and black pepper

Preheat grill. Wipe mushrooms and cut off stalks. Place mushrooms, gills facing up, on a non-stick baking sheet. Mix together garlic, parsley, water and stock powder and spread a little of this mixture over each mushroom cap. Place a few rings of pepper on each mushroom. Season generously with salt and pepper. Place baking sheet near the middle of oven. Grill mushrooms until they soften and the topping begins to sizzle (about 15 minutes). Serve piping hot on thin slices of brown toast.

Serves 4

glazed baby carrots

This method of cooking carrots emphasises their natural sweetness. If you keep a few packets of frozen baby carrots in the deep freeze at all times, you'll find it easy to get your daily dose of special vegetables.

750 ml (3 cups) fresh or frozen baby carrots
5 ml (1 tsp) turmeric
15 ml (1 tbsp) runny honey (see Cook's tips, page 23), or to taste
salt and milled black pepper

Cook carrots in plenty of boiling, salted water until tender. Drain well. Tip into a warmed dish, add turmeric and honey and toss well to combine. Season with salt and pepper and serve hot.

Serves 4

lemon garlic green beans

Once you've tasted green beans cooked this way, you'll be hooked. Do use the smallest, most tender beans you can find.

1 punnet (about 300 g) slim green beans
stock made with 500 ml (2 cups) boiling water and 10 ml (2 tsp) vegetable stock powder
1–2 cloves garlic, peeled and very finely chopped, to taste
2 ml (½ tsp) prepared English mustard
juice of 1 lemon
salt and milled black pepper

Top and tail beans. Bring stock to the boil in a saucepan, add beans and boil briskly for 5–10 minutes, until beans are just cooked (they should still retain a crisp bite). Drain immediately in a colander, then plunge into ice-cold water for 30 seconds to set the colour. Drain again and put into a warmed ceramic dish. In a separate jug, mix together garlic, mustard and lemon juice. Pour over warmed beans, toss well and season to taste with salt and pepper. Serve immediately.

Serves 4

red cabbage with apple

A homely dish with a beautiful colour and flavour. This is a good way to get your daily dose of bright red vegetables and fruit.

2 onions, finely chopped
3 cloves garlic, peeled and crushed
1 red cabbage, finely shredded
3 red apples, diced
30 ml (2 tbsp) soft brown sugar
30 ml (2 tbsp) red or white wine vinegar
salt and milled black pepper

Dry-fry onions and garlic *(see page xi)* in a large saucepan. When onions are soft, add cabbage, apples, sugar and vinegar. Reduce heat, cover and simmer gently for 30–40 minutes, adding more water if necessary. Season with salt and pepper and serve hot.

Serves 4

SEXY OPTIONS

Add 5 ml (1 tsp) caraway seeds and a handful of sultanas to the cabbage.

baby marrows provençal

Baby marrows taste so good baked in a tomato sauce, yet the recipe couldn't be simpler. These are equally nice eaten cold the next day.

1 punnet (about 350 g) baby marrows
1 tin (400 g) tomato and onion mix
30 ml (2 tbsp) tomato purée
2 cloves garlic, peeled and crushed
5 ml (1 tsp) vegetable stock powder
5 ml (1 tsp) sugar
30 ml (2 tbsp) chopped fresh oregano or 10 ml (2 tsp) dried oregano
salt and milled black pepper
fresh basil leaves, torn into pieces

Preheat oven to 180 °C. Top and tail baby marrows and cut into fairly thick slices. Put in a shallow ovenproof dish. In a separate bowl, mix together tomato and onion mix, tomato purée, garlic, stock powder, sugar and oregano. Season to taste with salt and pepper. Pour mixture over baby marrows and stir gently to combine. Bake, uncovered, for 20 minutes, or until baby marrows are just cooked. Serve hot or cold, scattered with torn fresh basil leaves.

Serves 4

main courses

curried brinjals with greek rice

Greek rice, also known as orzo, is actually pasta shaped like grains of rice. A good substitute is pasta rice (risoni), available in good supermarkets and Italian delicatessens.

2 large brinjals, cubed
10 small potatoes, halved
2 large onions, finely chopped
1 tin (400 g) chopped, peeled tomatoes
10 ml (2 tsp) medium curry powder
250 ml (1 cup) Greek rice
625 ml (2½ cups) water
salt and milled black pepper
10 ml (2 tsp) cornflour mixed with 45 ml (3 tbsp) water

TO SERVE
fruity chutney
chopped tomatoes
chopped green peppers
chopped spring onions

Preheat oven to 180 °C. Put all ingredients into a deep non-stick ovenproof dish, add cornflour paste and mix very well. Cover with a lid or foil and bake for 1 hour, stirring occasionally, until the Greek rice is cooked, adding a little more water or stock if necessary. Serve hot, and pass around separate bowls of chutney and chopped vegetables.

Serves 4–6

creamy mushroom pasta

This dish really does have a creamy taste and texture. I adore mushrooms and use them for cooking whenever I can.

2 onions, finely chopped
4 cloves garlic, peeled and crushed
30 ml (2 tbsp) chopped fresh parsley
10 ml (2 tsp) dried mixed Italian herbs
2 punnets (about 300 g each) large brown mushrooms, sliced
2 tins (400 g each) Denny Condensed Cream of Mushroom Soup
80 ml (⅓ cup) sherry
250 ml (1 cup) buttermilk
salt and milled black pepper
500 g tagliatelle
chopped fresh parsley, to garnish

Dry-fry onions and garlic (see page xi). When onions are soft and golden, add parsley, dried herbs and mushrooms. Cover, reduce heat and simmer for about 10 minutes, or until juices run and mushrooms are soft. Add tinned soup and sherry and simmer for another 3–5 minutes, stirring constantly. Remove sauce from heat and stir in buttermilk. Season to taste with salt and pepper. Meanwhile, cook tagliatelle in plenty of boiling, salted water. Drain in a colander and tip into a deep warmed bowl. Pour over sauce and mix together carefully. Sprinkle fresh parsley on top and serve piping hot.

Serves 4–6

SEXY OPTIONS

Dried wild mushrooms add a deep, rich flavour and a hint of real luxury to this sauce. They are available at selected greengrocers, delicatessens and farm stalls. Although they are pricey, you will only need a small handful. Before using dried mushrooms, soak in boiling water for 30 minutes, then rinse well to remove any grit.

VEGETABLES

artichoke and mushroom fettucine

Tinned artichoke hearts are expensive, but I always keep a few tins in the store cupboard because their delicate, astringent flavour adds a deliciously luxurious note to many vegetable dishes and salads.

2 onions, finely chopped
4 cloves garlic, peeled and crushed
1 tin (400 g) chopped, peeled tomatoes, drained
15 ml (1 tbsp) sugar
10 ml (2 tsp) dried mixed Italian herbs
30 ml (2 tbsp) tomato purée
250 ml (1 cup) white wine
2 punnets (about 300 g each) button mushrooms, halved
45 ml (3 tbsp) cornflour
250 ml (1 cup) fat-free milk
2 tins (400 g each) artichoke hearts, plus their juice
salt and milled black pepper
500 g fettucine

Dry-fry onions and garlic (*see page xi*). When onions are soft and golden, add tomatoes, sugar, dried herbs, tomato purée and wine and mix well. Stir in mushrooms. Cover saucepan, reduce heat and simmer until mushrooms are soft (about 20 minutes). Put cornflour in a teacup, add a little of the milk and mix to a smooth, runny paste. Add paste to mushroom sauce and cook over a low heat, stirring constantly to avoid lumps forming, until smooth and thickened. Cut each artichoke heart in half and add to sauce along with juice from tin and remaining milk. Season generously with salt and pepper. Meanwhile, cook fettucine in plenty of boiling, salted water. Drain in a colander and tip into a deep warmed bowl. Pour over the sauce and mix together carefully. Just before serving, grind over more black pepper.

Serves 4–6

sopa da fideos

Despite its name, which means 'noodle soup' in Spanish, this dish is really a thick, chunky stew that will warm you through on even the coldest of days.

1 packet (200 g) tomato and onion soya mince plus water to make up
3 onions, finely sliced
3 cloves garlic, peeled and crushed
500 g vermicelli
2 green peppers, finely chopped
6 ribs celery, trimmed and finely sliced
1 tin (400 g) whole kernel sweetcorn, drained
5–15 ml (1–3 tsp) chilli powder (see Cook's tips), to taste
3 tins (400 g each) chopped, peeled tomatoes
250 ml (1 cup) water
salt and milled black pepper
chopped fresh coriander

Cook soya mince with water as directed on the packet. Dry-fry onions and garlic (*see page xi*). When onions begin to brown, break vermicelli into short pieces and add to onions. Continue dry-frying until vermicelli turns golden brown. Add cooked soya mince and all remaining ingredients except coriander. Bring to the boil, stirring constantly. Reduce heat, cover and simmer gently for 30 minutes, stirring occasionally and adding more water if necessary (the texture should be very thick). Adjust seasoning. Serve in the pot, scattered with chopped fresh coriander.

COOK'S TIPS

x For an authentic flavour, this dish must be really hot and spicy, so add as much chilli powder as you can bear. Chilli powder is usually very hot, although its strength depends on the chillies that went into it. Some brands will tell you the strength, although with others you'll have to experiment to find out just how hot they are.

roast vegetable pasta

The jewel-like colours and concentrated flavours of oven-roasted vegetables make them ideal for feeding guests who are keen on vegetables.

2 red peppers
2 green peppers
2 yellow peppers
1 punnet (about 300 g) large brown mushrooms
1 punnet (about 350 g) baby marrows
2 large onions or 12 pickling onions
stock made with 250 ml (1 cup) boiling water and 5 ml (1 tsp) vegetable stock powder
5 cloves garlic, peeled and crushed
60 ml ($^{1}/_{4}$ cup) Worcestershire sauce
45 ml (3 tbsp) soft brown sugar
30 ml (2 tbsp) tomato sauce
10 ml (2 tsp) dried mixed herbs
salt and milled black pepper
500 g fusilli or other large pasta shape
fresh basil leaves, torn into pieces

Preheat oven to 200 °C. Trim and de-seed peppers and cut each one into 6–8 thick wedges. Wipe mushrooms and cut into quarters. Top and tail baby marrows and cut into 2 cm lengths. Cut each onion into 6 wedges. (If you're using pickling onions, peel and leave whole.) Line a deep roasting pan with a double thickness of tin foil and arrange the vegetables in a single layer on the foil. In a jug, combine stock, garlic, Worcestershire sauce, sugar, tomato sauce and dried herbs. Pour over vegetables and mix well to ensure that each piece is thoroughly coated. Season with salt and pepper. Place roasting dish near the top of the oven and bake until vegetables are tender and slightly charred and toasted at the edges (45–60 minutes). Check often and turn once or twice during cooking. Meanwhile, cook fusilli in plenty of boiling, salted water. Drain in a colander and tip into a deep warmed bowl. Pour over the roasted vegetables and their juices, and mix together carefully. Serve hot with a scattering of fresh basil.

Serves 4–6

SEXY OPTIONS

If you have a penchant for garlic, use 6–10 whole peeled cloves in addition to the crushed cloves. But don't forget to warn your guests to look out for them! Alternatively, place 1 or 2 whole, unpeeled heads of garlic among the vegetables. When roasted, the garlic turns soft and can be squeezed out of its skin. Don't be afraid — it has a much milder taste cooked this way.

penne with spinach and yoghurt sauce

This dish has a mild, fresh flavour and a lovely colour, and is ideal to serve in small portions as a starter before a rich dinner of fish or chicken.

1 bunch spinach
1 clove garlic, peeled and crushed
30 ml (2 tbsp) chopped fresh dill or 10 ml (2 tsp) dried dill
5 ml (1 tsp) vegetable stock powder
250 ml (1 cup) fat-free plain yoghurt
salt and milled black pepper
500 g penne

Pull stalks and any tough strands off spinach leaves and rinse very well to remove all traces of grit. Place wet leaves in a large pot over a medium heat (there will be enough water clinging to the leaves to cook the spinach). Add garlic, dill and stock powder, cover with a lid and cook, stirring and turning spinach occasionally, for 10–15 minutes, or until spinach is well wilted and most of the moisture has evaporated. Tip into a sieve and drain well, pressing down with a saucer or small plate to remove excess liquid. Turn onto a chopping board and chop roughly. Tip into a bowl, add yoghurt and mix well to combine. Season generously with salt and pepper. Meanwhile, cook penne in plenty of boiling, salted water. Drain in a colander and tip into a deep, warmed dish. Pour over sauce and mix together carefully. Serve hot.

Serves 4–6

double-quick tomato pasta

If you're in the mood for pasta but have only a few minutes to spare, this is the sauce for you. It's a good basic fat-free sauce that can be perked up with all sorts of interesting ingredients, so do keep a supply of it in the fridge or freezer.

2 tins (400 g each) tomato and onion mix
2 cloves garlic, peeled and crushed
10 ml (2 tsp) vegetable stock powder
15 ml (1 tbsp) dried mixed Italian herbs
5 ml (1 tsp) dried oregano
250 ml (1 cup) white wine
10 ml (2 tsp) sugar
5 ml (1 tsp) salt
500 g pasta
milled black pepper

Put all ingredients except salt, pepper and pasta into a saucepan and bring to the boil. Reduce heat and simmer, uncovered, until reduced and thickened (about 20 minutes), stirring occasionally. Season to taste with salt. Meanwhile, cook pasta in plenty of boiling, salted water. Drain in a colander and tip into a deep warmed bowl. Pour over the sauce and mix together carefully. Just before serving, grind over plenty of black pepper.

Serves 4–6

COOK'S TIPS

x Continue cooking the sauce until it is well thickened and use it for spreading over pizza bases.

SEXY OPTIONS

A handful of torn fresh basil leaves and a few drops of anchovy essence will add a Mediterranean flavour.

farfalle with pumpkin sauce

Any pasta shape can be used in this dish, but I think that farfalle, with its pretty butterfly shape, looks best with the delicate yellow sauce.

500 ml (2 cups) peeled and diced pumpkin
1 large onion, grated
125 ml ($^1/_2$ cup) water
15 ml (1 tbsp) paprika
5 ml (1 tsp) chicken stock powder
15 ml (1 tbsp) soft brown sugar
250 ml (1 cup) fat-free milk
30 ml (2 tbsp) fat-free milk powder
20 ml (4 tsp) cornflour
30 ml (2 tbsp) fat-free plain yoghurt
salt and milled black pepper
500 g farfalle

Put pumpkin and onion in a saucepan with the water. Bring to the boil, reduce heat, cover and simmer until pumpkin is very soft (about 1 hour). Drain well. Put into a food processor or blender and add paprika, stock powder, sugar, milk, milk powder and cornflour. Process to a fine purée. Return purée to rinsed-out pot and reheat, stirring constantly until thickened. Remove from the heat and stir in yoghurt. Season with salt and pepper. Reheat very gently, to warm through. Meanwhile, cook farfalle in plenty of boiling, salted water. Drain in a colander and tip into a deep warmed bowl. Pour over sauce and mix together carefully. Serve hot.

Serves 4–6

SEXY OPTION

Give the sauce a lift by stirring in 10 ml (2 tsp) finely grated orange zest and 5 ml (1 tsp) ground coriander when you add the yoghurt.

family favourites

The one rule we always hold fast to in the X Clinic is that the 'healthy' person should notice as few changes as possible to their normal way of life. So we have gone to the ends of the earth and asked thousands of people to find out what their families want most. After laughing almost ashamedly, they invariably come out with the most fatty of meals. This is normal! And, what's more, these are favourites because they have the most flavour and least resemble diet food. It is this comfort factor that the X Diet plans to bring back into the home, in a way that will satisfy even the most traditional of rumbling tummies, and no-one will notice why they are getting trimmer and filled with more energy! These recipes are as close to the real thing as possible, and don't be surprised if you get comments from friends, like 'Oh! I would love to have seconds, but I'm trying to slim down!' because they certainly look full of fat, but contain none at all.

x diet pizza

All the flavour and texture of a piping hot, chewy pizza, without the cheese or the olive oil!

BASE
625 ml (2½ cups) cake flour
5 ml (1 tsp) salt
5 ml (1 tsp) active dry yeast
15 ml (1 tbsp) sugar
250 ml (1 cup) fat-free milk
4 egg whites, lightly beaten

TOPPING
250 ml (1 cup) tomato purée
5 ml (1 tsp) dried mixed herbs
1 onion, grated
2 cloves garlic, peeled and crushed
1 punnet (about 300 g) large brown mushrooms, sliced
125 ml (½ cup) frozen sweetcorn kernels
3–4 fresh green chillies, de-seeded and finely chopped, to taste
2 green peppers, thinly sliced
4 tomatoes, thinly sliced

To make the base, sift flour and salt into a bowl and stir in yeast and sugar. Warm milk to just above blood temperature. Make a well in dry ingredients and pour in milk and beaten egg whites. Mix well to combine, then knead for 5 minutes until dough is smooth and elastic. Cover the bowl with a wet tea towel and leave to rise until doubled in size (about 1 hour). Preheat oven to 200 °C. Knock back dough and stretch it to about 30 x 40 cm. Put onto a non-stick baking tray. To make the topping, mix together tomato purée, dried herbs, onion and garlic. Spread mixture over pizza base to within 2 cm of edges. Arrange mushrooms, sweetcorn, chillies, pepper slices and tomato slices evenly over base. Bake for 25 minutes, or until base is well risen and golden at the edges. Serve hot with a green salad, or cold as a picnic lunch.

Serves 4–6

fish cakes

Children always like these fish cakes, and I think that grown-ups will appreciate them too!

4 large, floury potatoes, peeled and cubed
45 ml (3 tbsp) buttermilk
salt and milled black pepper
4 x 100 g haddock loins, poached and flaked (see Very Simple Haddock, page 53)
1 small onion, finely grated
45 ml (3 tbsp) finely chopped fresh parsley
pinch of grated nutmeg
2 egg whites, lightly beaten
250 ml (1 cup) Kellogg's Cornflakes Crumbs

Preheat oven to 200 °C. Cook potatoes in plenty of boiling, salted water until tender. Drain well, stir in buttermilk and mash to a smooth purée. Season generously with salt and pepper. Add flaked haddock, onion, parsley, nutmeg and egg whites and mix thoroughly. To make fish cakes, divide the mixture into equal-sized balls and shape into flattish rounds 2 cm thick. Roll each patty in crumbs, making sure that it is thickly and evenly coated. Put the patties onto a non-stick baking sheet and place in the middle of the oven. Bake patties until firm and golden brown. Serve with wedges of lemon and a bowl of tomato sauce or Tartare Sauce (see page 91).

Serves 4

COOK'S TIPS

x If you don't have buttermilk, mash the potatoes with a little of the milk in which you poached the haddock.

SEXY OPTIONS

Add 30 ml (2 tbsp) lemon juice and 15 ml (1 tbsp) grated lemon zest to the fish cakes. A tablespoon of very well drained, chopped capers will add extra bite.

no-guilt hamburgers

(See opposite page xii)

You can eat as many of these healthy burger patties as your heart desires, safe in the knowledge that they're not going to coat your arteries — or your thighs — with saturated animal fats. Serve with Golden Potato Wedges (*see page 30*) and Red Coleslaw (*see page 20*).

1 packet (200 g) savoury soya mince plus water to make up
2 large onions, finely chopped
3 slices brown bread, made into breadcrumbs
80 ml (1/3 cup) oat bran
15 ml (1 tbsp) dried mixed herbs
2 egg whites
45 ml (3 tbsp) Worcestershire sauce
30 ml (2 tbsp) tomato sauce
15 ml (1 tbsp) fruity chutney
salt and milled black pepper

TO SERVE
hamburger rolls
lettuce
sliced tomato, onion and gherkins
Tomato and Chilli Salsa (see page 6)

Cook soya mince with water as directed on the packet, adding an extra 10 minutes to the recommended cooking time. When soya mince is ready, add all remaining ingredients and mix well with a fork. Preheat oven to its hottest setting. To make patties, divide the mixture into eight balls and, with your hands, shape into flattish rounds 2–3 cm thick. Put the patties onto a non-stick baking sheet and bake for 10–15 minutes, until they begin to set and turn brown. Turn and cook the other side for a further 10–15 minutes. Split the hamburger rolls and place a hot patty inside each one. Garnish with lettuce, tomato, onion and gherkin and pass around the Tomato and Chilli Salsa.

Makes 8

COOK'S TIPS

x *Bread that is a day or two old is best for making breadcrumbs. If the mixture seems too sloppy to form into patties, add more crumbs to firm it up.*

vegetable lasagne

Here's a version of lasagne that doesn't even contain soya mince, yet it's no less tasty. When it was served at a dinner party alongside a real beef lasagne, even the men tucked in with gusto!

2 onions, chopped
3 cloves garlic, peeled and crushed
15 ml (1 tbsp) dried mixed Italian herbs
125 ml (1/2 cup) white wine
1 green pepper, finely chopped
45 ml (3 tbsp) tomato purée
1 tin (400 g) Pick 'n Pay Choice Cream of Tomato Soup
125 ml (1/2 cup) water
750 ml (3 cups) roughly chopped pumpkin or butternut
125 ml (1/2 cup) sun-dried tomatoes, soaked
salt and milled black pepper
500 g no-pre-cook lasagne sheets (see Cook's tips, page 42)
1 quantity white sauce (see page 91)

Dry-fry the onions until golden brown (*see page xi*). Add the garlic, herbs, wine and green pepper. Cook, stirring frequently, until green pepper is soft. Add the remaining ingredients except the lasagne sheets and white sauce and bring to the boil. Reduce heat and simmer gently, stirring occasionally, until the pumpkin is soft (about 20 minutes). Preheat oven to 180 °C. To assemble the lasagne, place a third of the vegetable sauce in a large, shallow ovenproof dish. Top with a layer of lasagne sheets, then a third of the white sauce. Add another layer of vegetable sauce, another of lasagne sheets, and so on, ending with a layer of white sauce. Bake for 20 minutes.

Serves 4

fat-free lasagne

This looks like a dauntingly long and complicated recipe but it really couldn't be simpler. Your friends will have a hard time telling this apart from the real thing.

1 packet (200 g) tomato and onion soya mince plus water to make up
2 onions, finely chopped
125 ml ($1/2$ cup) fresh basil leaves, torn into small pieces
30 ml (2 tbsp) dried mixed Italian herbs
10 ml (2 tsp) vegetable or beef stock powder
4 cloves garlic, peeled and crushed
1 punnet (about 300 g) large brown mushrooms, sliced
250 ml (1 cup) red wine
2 tins (400 g each) chopped, peeled tomatoes, drained
125 ml ($1/2$ cup) tomato purée
15 ml (1 tbsp) Bisto gravy powder
30 ml (2 tbsp) chutney
45 ml (3 tbsp) Worcestershire sauce
500 g no-pre-cook lasagne sheets
breadcrumbs, for sprinkling

WHITE SAUCE
1 l (4 cups) fat-free milk
45 ml (3 tbsp) cornflour
60 ml (4 tbsp) water
10 ml (2 tsp) salt
10 ml (2 tsp) milled black pepper
5 ml (1 tsp) prepared English mustard
15 ml (1 tbsp) sherry
1 bunch spring onions, finely chopped
45 ml (3 tbsp) soft brown sugar
1 sachet (15 g) Cubb's Cheese and Onion Party Dip powder
5 ml (1 tsp) cayenne pepper, or to taste

Preheat oven to 180 °C. To make mince sauce, cook soya mince with water as directed on the packet. Meanwhile, dry-fry onions (see page xi) until golden and softened. Add basil, dried herbs, stock powder, garlic and mushrooms. Reduce heat, cover and simmer until mushroom juices begin to run (about 10 minutes). Add cooked soya mince and mix well. Stir in wine, tomatoes, tomato purée, Bisto, chutney and Worcestershire sauce. Bring sauce to the boil, then reduce heat and cook, stirring frequently, until the sauce thickens and turns a deep, rich red (about 30 minutes). To make white sauce, heat milk in a saucepan. In a teacup, mix cornflour and water to a smooth, runny paste. Whisk paste into hot milk. Add salt, pepper, mustard, sherry, spring onions, sugar, dip powder and cayenne pepper to taste. Cook over a low heat, stirring constantly, until thickened. To assemble lasagne, place a third of the mince sauce in a large, shallow ovenproof dish. Top with a single layer of dry lasagne sheets. Pour over a third of the white sauce. Then add another layer of mince sauce, another of lasagne sheets, and so on, ending with a layer of white sauce. Sprinkle generously with breadcrumbs and bake for 20 minutes. Serve with a fresh spinach salad.

Serves 4–6

COOK'S TIPS

x For best results, use no-pre-cook lasagne sheets, now available in most supermarkets. This type of lasagne becomes soft by soaking up liquid from the sauce while it's in the oven. It should therefore be covered with plenty of wet sauce, otherwise it will remain hard in places even after prolonged cooking. For best results, dip each sheet in hot water before using and leave the assembled dish to stand for 20–30 minutes before baking.

x Although the dip powder is not low in fat on its own, when added to the sauce it works out at less than 1 g fat per 100 g sauce.

SEXY OPTIONS

Replace the soya mince and water with 500 g skinned, deboned chicken breasts, minced, and dry-fry with the onions. This makes a creamy chicken lasagne — another favourite no-one can refuse!

mexican chilli

Make an enormous pot of this fiery chilli to serve to hungry friends on a cold winter's night. If you've never been keen on soya mince, this is the one dish that is likely to turn you into a life-long devotee!

1 packet (200 g) tomato and onion soya mince plus water to make up
2 tins (400 g each) chopped, peeled tomatoes
125 ml (½ cup) tomato purée
2 onions, chopped
1 red pepper and 1 green pepper, finely chopped
1–3 large mild fresh chillies, de-seeded and finely chopped, to taste (see Cook's tips)
30 ml (2 tbsp) chilli flakes, or to taste
5 ml (1 tsp) dried oregano
10 ml (2 tsp) ground cumin
2 ml (½ tsp) cinnamon
pinch of allspice
pinch of ground cloves
1 tin (400 g) kidney beans, rinsed and drained
salt and milled black pepper
chopped fresh coriander

TOPPINGS
1 bunch spring onions, finely chopped
shredded lettuce
Tomato and Chilli Salsa (see page 6)
fat-free plain yoghurt

Cook soya mince with water as directed on the packet. Leave to stand for 5 minutes. Add all remaining ingredients except beans, seasoning and coriander and bring to the boil. Reduce heat, cover and simmer for 1 hour, stirring frequently and adding more water if mixture seems too dry. Add beans and cook, uncovered, for a further 25 minutes. Season to taste with salt and pepper. Serve hot on a bed of rice, garnished with fresh coriander and with toppings passed around in separate bowls.

Serves 6

COOK'S TIPS

x *Make Mexican Chilli the night before in order to allow the flavours to develop. In fact, the longer this dish is allowed to stand, the better it seems to taste.*

x *Try to find the large, mild chillies known as jalapeño peppers to use in this dish. If these aren't available, green chillies will do. Always remove the seeds from chillies before adding them to a dish, as these are the hottest part, and wash your hands thoroughly, as the juice will burn if it comes near your eyes, nose or mouth.*

crispy 'fried' fish

There's not a drop of oil in these crumbed fish fillets, but they are crunchy and golden on the outside and soft and succulent within. For best results, use really fresh fish.

60 ml (¼ cup) cake flour
salt and milled black pepper
2 egg whites, lightly beaten
250 ml (1 cup) Kellogg's Cornflakes Crumbs
4 x 100 g firm white fish fillets
lemon wedges

Preheat oven to 200 °C. Line a baking sheet with tin foil. Put flour in a wide, shallow dish and season generously with salt and pepper. Put egg whites in another shallow dish and crumbs in a third. Dip a fish fillet in flour, making sure that it is evenly coated. Shake off excess, then dip in egg white. Finely coat fillet in crumbs, pressing down well to ensure that it is evenly coated. Repeat with remaining fillets. Place fish on lined baking sheet and bake for 10 minutes (there is no need to turn them) until golden brown and cooked through. Serve with wedges of lemon and Golden Potato Wedges (see page 30).

Serves 4

spaghetti bolognese

(See opposite)
A very light version of a favourite family supper. Serve this substantial dish with a huge bowl of green salad and some crusty Garlic Bread (*see page 5*) and no one will suspect that it's the fat-free version.

1 packet (200 g) tomato and onion soya mince plus water to make up
2 onions, finely chopped
2 large carrots, finely chopped
2 ribs celery, finely sliced
1 punnet (about 300 g) button mushrooms, sliced
3 cloves garlic, peeled and crushed
125 ml ($\frac{1}{2}$ cup) red wine
1 tin (400 g) Pick 'n Pay Choice Cream of Tomato Soup
80 ml ($\frac{1}{3}$ cup) tomato purée
7 ml (1 heaped tsp) vegetable stock powder
30 ml (2 tbsp) soy sauce
30 ml (2 tbsp) dried mixed Italian herbs
salt
10 ml (2 tsp) milled black pepper
fresh basil leaves, torn into pieces
500 g spaghetti

Cook soya mince with water as directed on the packet. Meanwhile, in a separate saucepan, dry-fry onions (*see page xi*) until soft and golden. Add carrots, celery, mushrooms, garlic and wine and cook for 10 minutes, or until vegetables are slightly softened and mushroom juices begin to run. Stir in prepared soya mince along with tomato soup, tomato purée, stock powder, soy sauce and dried herbs. Season to taste with salt and pepper. Reduce heat and simmer very gently, uncovered, for 30 minutes. Meanwhile, cook spaghetti in plenty of boiling, salted water. Drain in a colander and tip into a deep warmed bowl. Pour over the sauce. Just before serving, scatter with fresh basil leaves and grind over some more black pepper.

Serves 4–6

ostrich steak and 'sour cream' potatoes

4 large baking potatoes
1 packet (about 20 stalks) fresh chives
500 ml (2 cups) buttermilk
4 ostrich fillet steaks, with no visible fat

Preheat oven to 200 °C. Scrub potatoes, rub each wet potato with salt and cut a slit in each one. Bake for 45–60 minutes, until cooked through. Meanwhile, make the 'sour cream'. Use kitchen scissors to snip the chives into the smallest pieces you can. Mix into the buttermilk and leave for as long as possible, for the flavours to develop. Heat a heavy skillet until very hot. Put ostrich steaks into the skillet and cook for about 10 minutes on each side, turning frequently to prevent them from sticking. Squeeze open the potatoes, pour over plenty of chive buttermilk and serve with the ostrich fillet.

Serves 4

SEXY OPTIONS

All kinds of low-fat sauces, such as mustards, chilli sauces and tomato sauce, can be doused over the ostrich fillet.

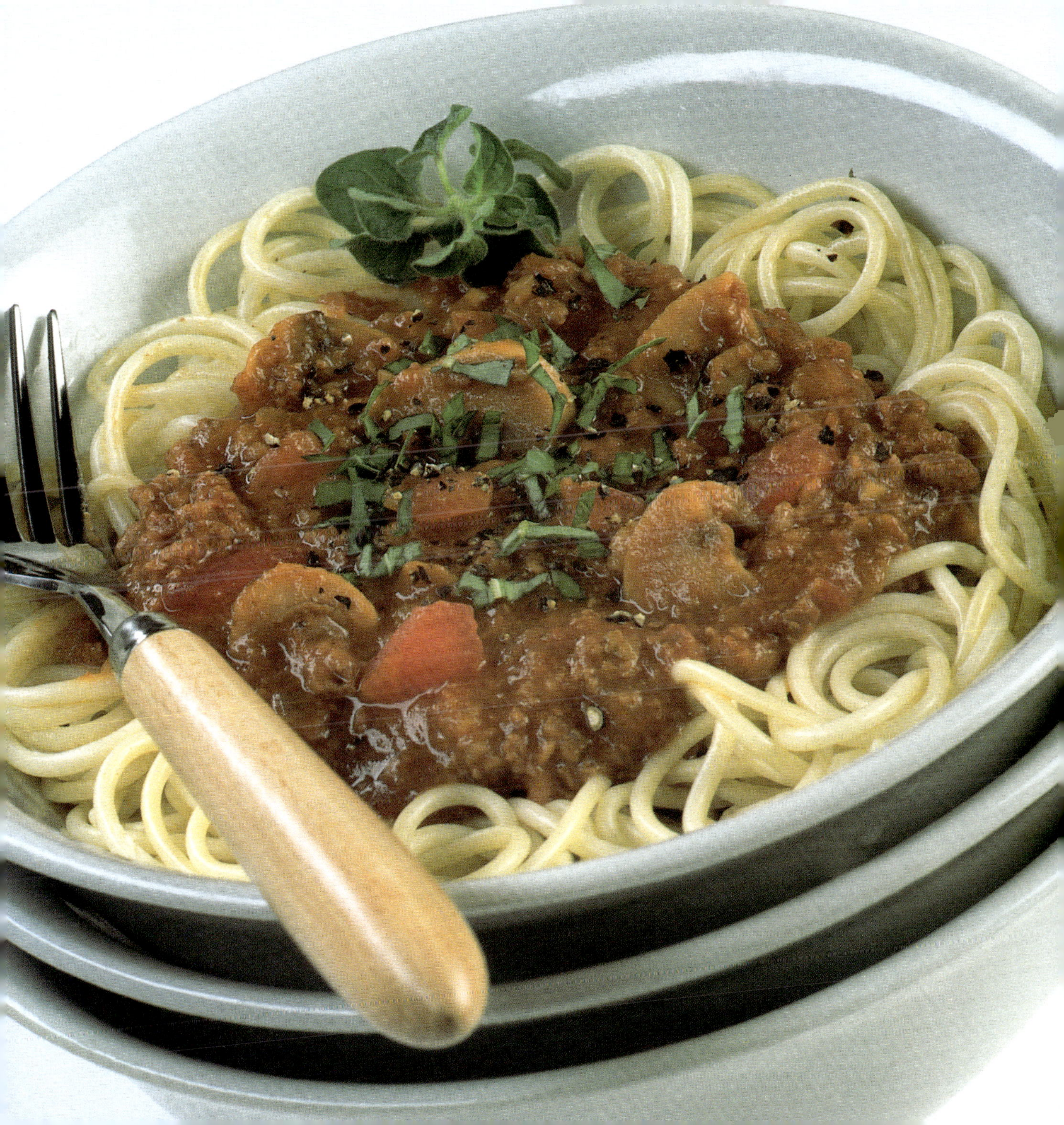

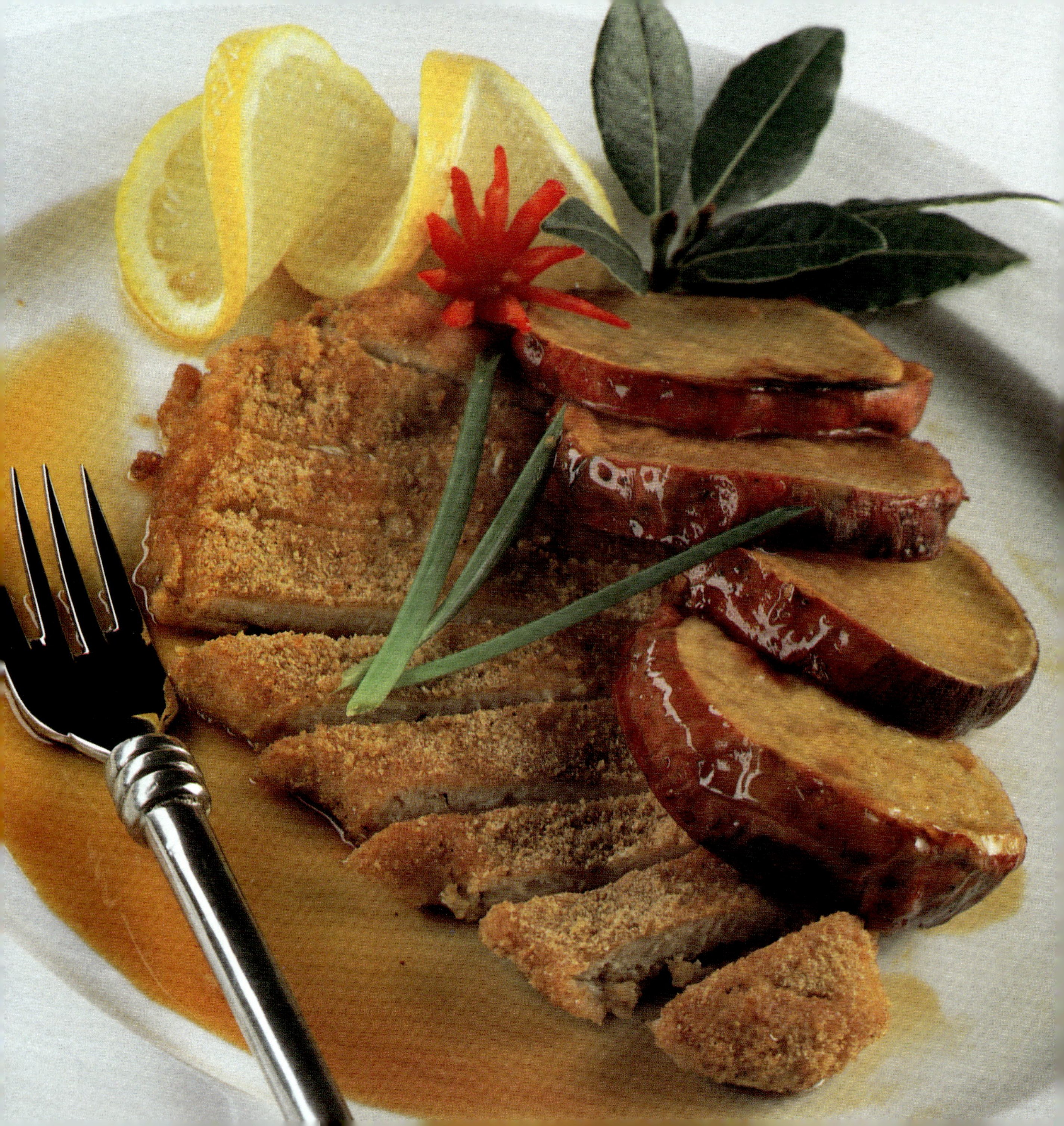

bobotie

1 packet (200 g) soya mince plus water to make up
1 slice bread
125 ml ($\frac{1}{2}$ cup) fat-free milk
3 onions, finely chopped
2 cloves garlic, peeled and crushed
10 ml (2 tsp) hot curry powder
10 ml (2 tsp) ground cumin
10 ml (2 tsp) ground coriander
30 ml (2 tbsp) brandy
juice of 2 lemons
125 ml ($\frac{1}{2}$ cup) seedless raisins
30 ml (2 tbsp) peach chutney
15 ml (1 tbsp) smooth apricot jam
30 ml (2 tbsp) turmeric
salt and milled black pepper

TOPPING
3 egg whites
125 ml ($\frac{1}{2}$ cup) fat-free milk
10 fresh bay leaves or lemon leaves

Preheat oven to 180 °C. Cook soya mince with water as directed on the packet. Soak the bread in the milk. Meanwhile, dry-fry the onions with the garlic (*see page xi*) until browned. Add curry powder, ground cumin and ground coriander and stir. When the spices begin to stick, add the brandy all at once, to create a hot, sticky steam that will 'open' the spices. Add the soya mince to the onion mixture. Break up the bread and stir in, until well combined. Add the rest of the ingredients and transfer to an ovenproof dish. To make the topping, beat together the egg whites and milk and pour over the mince. Crush the bay leaves or lemon leaves between your fingers, to release the fragrance, and push into the bobotie randomly. (The more leaves you use the better.) Bake for 30 minutes, or until the custard has set. Serve with turmeric or saffron rice and a selection of sambals (*see Sexy options*).

Serves 4

SEXY OPTIONS

A good selection of sambals to go with your bobotie should include sliced banana, chutney (your favourite type), chopped peppers, chopped onion, chopped tomato, stewed apricots, stewed prunes, fat-free plain yoghurt.

chicken schnitzels

(See opposite)
4 sweet potatoes
45 ml (3 tbsp) runny honey, warmed (see Cook's Tips, page 23)
2 skinned, deboned chicken breasts
2 egg whites
125 ml ($\frac{1}{2}$ cup) fat-free milk
125 ml ($\frac{1}{2}$ cup) Kellogg's Cornflakes Crumbs
chicken spice, to taste
salt and milled black pepper
lemon wedges

Preheat oven to 180 °C. Scrub sweet potatoes and brush with honey. Bake for 1 hour. Cut each chicken breast in half, across the grain, and use the smooth side of a meat tenderizer or a wooden rolling pin to flatten out each half. Beat together egg whites and milk. Dip each chicken schnitzel into the egg white mixture. Put the crumbs into a shallow dish and season well with chicken spice, salt and pepper. Dip the chicken into the crumbs, to coat both sides well. Place carefully into a roasting bag, seal and bake in the oven with the sweet potatoes for a further 15 minutes. Serve with lemon wedges.

Serves 4

FAMILY FAVOURITES 45

bangers and mash

To make these special X Diet bangers, you need a butcher that you can truly trust to do exactly what you ask him to do, otherwise you may end up with hidden fat.

400 g fat-free chicken bangers (see Cook's tips)
8 potatoes
60 ml (4 tbsp) buttermilk
20 ml (1 heaped tbsp) chopped fresh parsley
salt and milled black pepper
30 ml (2 tbsp) Bisto gravy powder
500 ml (2 cups) water
15 ml (1 tbsp) chopped fresh thyme
15 ml (1 tbsp) chopped fresh rosemary
15 ml (1 tbsp) chopped fresh oregano
15 ml (1 tbsp) brown sugar
125 ml (1/2 cup) red wine or 45 ml (3 tbsp) port

Preheat oven to 180 °C. Prick each chicken banger with a fork, place in a roasting bag and seal. Bake for about 30 minutes, until browned. Meanwhile, peel and cube potatoes and cook in boiling, salted water until tender (about 25 minutes). Drain, add buttermilk, parsley, salt and pepper, and mash well. To make gravy, mix Bisto powder with the water and pour into a saucepan. Add remaining ingredients and cook over a medium heat, stirring, until thickened. Serve the bangers and mash with plenty of gravy poured over the top.

COOK'S TIPS

x   Tell the butcher that you want bangers made with pure chicken breast fillet, and NOTHING ELSE — no skin, no fat. With this, your butcher should mix the usual rusk and herbs, but a bit more than usual because there is no fat to 'bring out the flavour'. The butcher might be reluctant to do this, out of concern for his reputation for creating his usual 'tasty' (and fatty) sausages. Tell him that you will be cooking them in a special way, and serving them with nice sauces and gravies. If you can really trust your butcher, he can be assured that you will be back for more!

chicken stew

A one-pot meal that the whole family will love, especially the cook: once you've put all the ingredients in the pot, you can relax for an hour while the stew simmers to perfection.

4 onions, chopped
4 skinned, deboned chicken breasts, sliced
15 ml (1 tbsp) chopped fresh thyme
15 ml (1 tbsp) chopped fresh rosemary
5 ml (1 tsp) mixed dried herbs
250 ml (1 cup) white wine
1 tin (400 g) tomato and onion mix
10 ml (2 tsp) chicken stock powder
500 ml (2 cups) boiling water
4 potatoes, scrubbed and cubed
250 ml (1 cup) carrots
250 ml (1 cup) broccoli
250 ml (1 cup) peas
250 ml (1 cup) pearl barley
45 ml (3 tbsp) mild chutney
salt and milled black pepper

Preheat oven to 200 °C. Dry-fry onions with the chicken pieces and herbs (*see page xi*). When browned, add the rest of the ingredients, stir and cover. Bake for about 1 hour, stirring occasionally. Serve piping hot.

Serves 4

vegetable curry

Although Coca-Cola may seem an unusual ingredient, the sugar in the cola raises the temperature high enough for the spices to 'open' (release their flavours), which stock alone is not able to do.

1 packet (200 g) savoury soya mince plus water to make up
3 onions, chopped
3 cloves garlic, peeled and crushed
10 ml (2 tsp) mild curry powder
10 ml (2 tsp) ground cumin
10 ml (2 tsp) ground coriander
125 ml ($^1/_2$ cup) Coca-Cola
45 ml (3 tbsp) brandy
45 ml (3 tbsp) garam masala
2 potatoes, peeled and cubed
250 ml (1 cup) frozen carrots
250 ml (1 cup) frozen peas

Cook soya mince with water as directed on the packet. Meanwhile, dry-fry the onions (*see page xi*). When the onions are browned, add the garlic and the spices (except garam masala). When the spices begin to stick and the pan is very hot, add the Coca-Cola to create a sticky, hot steam. Add the soya mince to the onion mixture, along with the remaining ingredients. Reduce the heat and simmer gently for 30 minutes. Serve with turmeric or saffron rice (*see Sexy options*).

Serves 4

SEXY OPTIONS

To make turmeric rice, cook rice as directed, but add 10 ml (2 tsp) turmeric to the cooking water.

To make saffron rice, soak a couple of saffron threads in 30 ml (2 tbsp) water and add the saffron and soaking water to the rice while cooking. Saffron is made from the stamens of a particular type of crocus, and is the most expensive spice in the world. Not much is needed, however, to lend a dish its very special taste and fragrance.

mexican pasta casserole

Make this spicy, sustaining dish at least 12 hours before you want to serve it, because it takes time for the flavours to develop fully.

1 packet (200 g) savoury soya mince plus water to make up
3 large onions, chopped
3 cloves garlic, peeled and crushed
2 green peppers, chopped
500 g pasta shells
250 ml (1 cup) tomato purée
1 punnet (about 300 g) whole button mushrooms
15 ml (1 tbsp) soft brown sugar
30 ml (2 tbsp) Worcestershire sauce
1 tin (400 g) whole kernel sweetcorn, drained
125 ml ($^1/_2$ cup) sherry
1–3 fresh green chillies, de-seeded and finely chopped, to taste
salt and milled black pepper

Cook soya mince with water as directed on the packet, but simmer for an extra 15 minutes. Meanwhile, dry-fry onions, garlic and green pepper (*see page xi*) until softened. While vegetables are cooking, put the noodles in plenty of boiling, salted water and cook for 5–8 minutes only (they should be slightly under-cooked). Drain thoroughly in a colander, then add to cooked vegetables. Remove pot from heat and stir in cooked soya mince and all remaining ingredients. Season with salt and pepper to taste. Tip into a deep non-stick ovenproof dish and cover tightly with foil. Leave to cool then refrigerate overnight. The next day, preheat oven to 160 °C and bake, covered, for 1$^1/_2$ hours, stirring every 20 minutes or so to prevent the mixture from sticking. Serve hot with a crisp green salad.

Serves 4–6

macaroni 'cheese'

There can scarcely be a more cheesy dish than the traditional macaroni cheese, but this version is the exception — it contains no cheese at all! What it does have, however, is plenty of flavour.

250 ml (1 cup) finely grated butternut
2 spring onions, finely chopped
2 ml (½ tsp) prepared English mustard
5 ml (1 tsp) vegetable stock powder
5 ml (1 tsp) soy sauce
15 ml (1 tbsp) fruity chutney
5 ml (1 tsp) dried dill or oregano
5 ml (1 tsp) cayenne pepper, or to taste
1 punnet (about 300 g) button mushrooms, sliced
30 ml (2 tbsp) fat-free milk powder
1 l (4 cups) fat-free milk
30 ml (2 tbsp) cake flour
15 ml (1 tbsp) cornflour
salt and milled black pepper
2 tomatoes, finely sliced
80 ml (⅓ cup) buttermilk
15 ml (1 tbsp) paprika
500 g macaroni

Preheat oven to 180 °C. Dry-fry grated butternut and spring onion in a large saucepan (*see page xi*). When vegetables are soft (about 10 minutes), tip into a food processor or blender and liquidise to a smooth purée, adding a little water if the mixture seems too dry. Pour the purée back into the saucepan and stir in mustard, stock powder, soy sauce, chutney, dill or oregano and cayenne pepper. Dry-fry mushrooms. Reserve. Dissolve milk powder in milk. Put a little of this milk into a teacup, add cornflour and cake flour and mix to a smooth, runny paste. Add flour paste to butternut sauce along with remaining milk and cook gently, whisking constantly to prevent lumps forming. When sauce is thickened and smooth, stir in reserved mushrooms and season with salt and pepper. Meanwhile, cook macaroni in plenty of boiling, salted water. Drain well in a colander and stir into hot sauce. Mix carefully to ensure that pasta is well coated. Tip into a deep non-stick ovenproof dish and arrange tomato slices in an overlapping pattern on top. Pour buttermilk over tomatoes, sprinkle with paprika and bake for 20–25 minutes, or until golden brown. Serve hot with a crispy green salad.

Serves 4–6

SEXY OPTIONS

Add a cup or two of steamed broccoli florets to the macaroni cheese. Don't overcook the broccoli — it should be slightly crunchy when it goes in to bake as it will finish cooking in the oven.

If you're giving a dinner party for vegetarian friends and would like to make a more substantial dish, layer the macaroni with other cooked vegetables, such as carrots, baby marrows, dry-fried brinjal slices, spinach and slices of baked butternut. You may need to make a little extra white sauce to coat the vegetables thoroughly.

fish & seafood

𝓕ish and seafood are wonderful parts of this eating plan, for many reasons. Firstly, fish has always been bottom on people's lists of favourites, because we really only want it fried so that it doesn't taste too 'fishy'. Aware of this, we have designed ways to incorporate rich and creamy sauces to accompany these gems, as well as cooking methods that will get your most ardent fish-hater coming back for more. The fish used in these recipes are all 'fat-free' fish, mainly the firm, white kinds — hake, kingklip, sole, kabeljou, haddock and other white linefish which can be used in most of the dishes. With fish becoming the most healthy and trendy option on anyone's menu, fishmongers are scattered everywhere, so you don't need to be near the sea to share in its delights!

Shellfish have always, unfortunately, been associated with high cholesterol levels. The good news is that this rule only applies to a very small section of the population, and the other cholesterol sufferers need not worry about this any longer. Syndrome X does not respond to the cholesterol in food but rather to the saturated fats in animal products, which we are careful to leave well out of these recipes! So, as a special family meal, or dinner-party favourite, trade the red meat or roast lamb for a fresh selection of delicious shellfish dishes — same cost, more excitement!

pasta marinara

One of the cornerstones of the X Diet is never, ever, to feel as if you're depriving yourself of life's delicious foods — and how could anyone feel deprived, tucking into a plate of piping-hot prawns, mussels and pasta?

2 tins (400 g each) tomato and onion mix
1 clove garlic, peeled and crushed
5 ml (1 tsp) vegetable stock powder
125 ml ($1/2$ cup) white wine
5 ml (1 tsp) salt
15 ml (1 tbsp) dried mixed Italian herbs or 30 ml (2 tbsp) chopped fresh oregano
6 raw prawns in their shells, fresh or frozen
6 mussels in their shells (see Cook's tips)
500 g tagliatelle
10 ml (2 tsp) milled black pepper

Put tomato and onion mix, garlic, stock powder, wine, salt and herbs into a saucepan and bring to the boil. Turn down the heat and simmer gently, uncovered, for 30 minutes, stirring occasionally. Add frozen prawns and mussels and simmer for a further 3–4 minutes. Meanwhile, cook tagliatelle in plenty of boiling, salted water. Drain pasta in a colander and tip into a deep warmed bowl. Pour over sauce and mix together carefully. Just before serving, grind over plenty of black pepper.

Serves 4–6

COOK'S TIPS

* Fresh, frozen or tinned mussels in their shells may be used in this recipe. If using fresh mussels, scrub and rinse well to remove all traces of grit. Discard any shells that are already open and that don't close when tapped — they are already dead and should not be eaten. After cooking, discard any whose shells have not opened. Fresh clams in their shells should be treated in the same way.

SEXY OPTION

Add 45 ml (3 tbsp) chopped fresh fennel or dill and 5 ml (1 tsp) finely grated lemon zest to the sauce when you put in the seafood.

For an extra-luxurious marinara, stir in a few teaspoons of caviar when you bring the pasta to the table.

prawn pilaff

This is one of my favourite seafood recipes. It's a good dish for a light weekend lunch, and can be prepared with the minimum of fuss.

375 ml ($1^1/2$ cups) long-grain rice
16 raw prawns, shelled
2 onions, finely chopped
1 green pepper, finely chopped
2 tomatoes, chopped
5 ml (1 tsp) turmeric
juice of 2 lemons
5 ml (1 tsp) cayenne pepper, or to taste
salt and milled black pepper

Cook rice as directed on the packet. Keep warm. Plunge prawns into boiling salted water and cook for 1 minute. Drain and reserve. Dry-fry onions and green pepper (see page xi). When onions are soft and golden, remove from heat and add tomatoes, turmeric, lemon juice and cayenne pepper. Add cooked rice and prawns and toss until well combined. Season with salt and pepper. Serve hot with a green salad.

Serves 4

millionaire's fish pie

This is a sophisticated (though fat-free) version of a very homely dish.

1 onion, finely chopped
1 punnet (about 300 g) large brown mushrooms, sliced
30 ml (2 tbsp) sherry
15 ml (1 tbsp) brandy
5 ml (1 tsp) salt
5 ml (1 tsp) milled black pepper
500 ml (2 cups) fat-free milk
1 bay leaf
4 x 100 g firm white fish fillets, fresh or frozen
20 ml (4 tsp) cornflour
45 ml (3 tbsp) water
250 ml (1 cup) frozen mixed shellfish or marinara mix
125 ml (½ cup) chopped fresh parsley

TOPPING
8 large potatoes, peeled, cubed and boiled
125-250 ml (½-1 cup) buttermilk
salt and milled black pepper
1 egg white, beaten
30 ml (2 tbsp) fat-free milk

Preheat oven to 180 °C. Dry-fry onion (see page xi). When onion is softened and golden, add mushrooms, sherry, brandy, salt and pepper. Reduce heat and simmer until mushrooms are soft and the juices begin to run. Add milk and bay leaf. As sauce returns to the boil, add whole fish fillets and poach over a medium heat until just cooked (about 10 minutes; the fish will turn opaque and flake easily). Using a slotted spoon, remove fish and reserve. In a teacup, mix cornflour and water to a smooth, runny paste. Add paste to hot sauce and cook over a low heat, stirring constantly to prevent lumps forming, until smooth and thickened. Tip in the shellfish, stir well and allow to simmer gently for 3–4 minutes. Remove from heat, discard bay leaf and stir in parsley. To make topping, mash potatoes, adding enough buttermilk to make a smooth, thick mash. Season to taste with salt and pepper. Place reserved fish fillets in a non-stick ovenproof dish and pour over hot shellfish sauce. Cover with mashed potato. Using the tines of a fork, mark a herringbone pattern on the surface of the potato. Mix together beaten egg white and milk and brush over potato. Bake, uncovered, for 20 minutes, or until topping is golden brown. Serve with Lemon Garlic Green Beans (see page 34).

Serves 4–6

COOK'S TIPS

* Frozen hake or kingklip fillets work perfectly well in this dish. There is no need to thaw them before poaching, but remember that they will take slightly longer to cook than fresh fish fillets.

poached sole

This dish couldn't be simpler — yet it has an incredible flavour. Many of my patients regard it as a staple.

250 ml (1 cup) hot water
20 ml (4 tsp) vegetable stock powder
4 whole sole, skinned

Mix together water and stock, pour into a large non-stick frying pan and bring mixture to the boil. Put in the sole (2 at a time if they are large). Reduce heat and cook for exactly 2 minutes on each side. Remove with a slotted spoon and place on a warmed platter. Serve hot with Crispy Potato Croquettes (see page 30).

Serves 4

sole with three-mustard and dill sauce

This is a wonderful way of cooking fresh sole, as the tin foil parcels prevent the fish from drying out. I like to serve these with boiled new potatoes, wedges of lemon and a green salad of rocket, watercress and Crispy Croûtons (see page 12).

4 whole sole, skinned (see Cook's tips)
5 ml (1 tsp) salt
5 ml (1 tsp) milled black pepper
juice of 1 lemon
80 ml (1/3 cup) white wine
20 ml (4 tsp) prepared English mustard
20 ml (4 tsp) Dijon mustard
20 ml (4 tsp) American mustard
1 small onion, grated
30 ml (2 tbsp) soft brown sugar
125 ml (1/2 cup) water
45 ml (3 tbsp) chopped fresh dill or 15 ml (1 tbsp) dried dill

Preheat oven to 160 °C. Cut out 4 squares of tin foil, lay shiny side up and place a sole on each one. Mix together salt, pepper, lemon juice and half the wine. Sprinkle this mixture evenly over the sole fillets. Wrap each fillet tightly in its foil parcel and place on a baking sheet. Bake for 20 minutes. While fish is baking, put the three mustards, onion, sugar, water and remaining wine in a saucepan and simmer gently until onion is softened (about 10 minutes). Remove from heat and stir in dill. Unwrap sole parcels, transfer fish to serving plates and pour sauce over. Serve immediately with boiled new potatoes and a green salad.

Serves 4

wine-baked asparagus kingklip

A quick and easy way of cooking kingklip, which is one of my favourite fish. If you don't have kingklip, use hake fillets instead — even the frozen ones will do. This dish is best served with rice and steamed green beans.

1 tin (400 g) asparagus cuts, plus their juice
4 x 100 g kingklip fillets
125 ml (1/2 cup) white wine
salt and milled black pepper
1 onion, finely chopped
250 ml (1 cup) fat-free milk
45 ml (3 tbsp) fat-free milk powder
20 ml (4 tsp) cornflour
chopped fresh parsley

Preheat oven to 180 °C. Drain asparagus, reserving liquid. Arrange fish fillets in a single layer in a non-stick ovenproof dish. Scatter asparagus over the top. Pour over the wine and season generously with salt and pepper. Cover dish tightly with tin foil and bake for 15–20 minutes, or until fish turns opaque and flakes easily. Meanwhile, dry-fry onion (see page xi) until soft and golden. Add reserved juice from asparagus. In a jug, combine milk, milk powder and cornflour and whisk until smooth and free of lumps. Add milk mixture to saucepan and cook over a low heat, stirring constantly, until sauce is smooth and thick. Remove fish from dish with a slotted spoon and arrange on a warmed platter. Add baked asparagus and cooking juices to sauce and mix carefully. Adjust seasoning, pour sauce over fish fillets and scatter with chopped parsley.

Serves 4

COOK'S TIPS

x You can use either whole sole, with just the skin and head removed, or ask your fishmonger to cut each fish into separate fillets. If you can't find fresh sole, use the best quality frozen sole fillets you can find. Defrost the fillets for 30 minutes and pat dry before wrapping in foil.

mushroom and tuna bake

A good dish for a Sunday-night family supper. Even children who loathe all other types of fish will enjoy this thick and hearty tuna bake.

500 g pasta shells
1 onion, finely chopped
2 cloves garlic, peeled and crushed
1 punnet (about 300 g) button mushrooms, sliced
1 green pepper, finely sliced
45 ml (3 tbsp) cornflour
500 ml (2 cups) fat-free milk
3 tomatoes, chopped
2 tins (200 g each) tuna in brine, drained and flaked
5 ml (1 tsp) turmeric

Preheat oven to 160 °C. Cook pasta shells in plenty of boiling salted water. Drain in a colander and reserve. Meanwhile, dry-fry onion and garlic (see page xi). When onion is soft and golden, add mushrooms and green pepper. Reduce heat, cover and cook gently until peppers are soft and mushroom juices begin to run. Put cornflour in a teacup and add just enough of the milk to make a smooth, runny paste. Add paste to onions and mushrooms along with remaining milk. Cook over a low heat, stirring constantly, until sauce is thick and smooth. Stir in tomatoes and tuna and season to taste with salt and black pepper. Carefully fold in reserved pasta shells. Tip mixture into a deep non-stick ovenproof dish and sprinkle with turmeric. Bake uncovered for 10–15 minutes. Serve hot with a green salad.

Serves 4

very simple haddock

This dish lives up to its name — it is indeed a doddle to make. This is a delicious way to cook fish, as there is none of that off-putting fishy aroma.

500 ml (2 cups) fat-free milk
4 x 100 g haddock loins, fresh or frozen (see Cook's tips)
salt and milled black pepper

Heat milk in a saucepan and put in the haddock loins. Cover pot, reduce heat and poach fish very gently until it is cooked through and flakes easily with a fork (about 10–15 minutes). Be careful not to overcook the fish or allow the milk to boil vigorously: it should barely simmer. Remove haddock and drain well. Pour some of the poaching liquid over the fish and season well with salt and pepper. Serve with fluffy mashed potatoes and Creamed Spinach (see page 26).

Serves 4

COOK'S TIPS

x There is no need to defrost frozen haddock before cooking: simply cook for an extra 5 minutes.

greek-style hake

A simple dish with a fresh taste. Serve with Curried Brinjals with Greek Rice *(see Cook's tips, page 35).*

2 onions, finely sliced
2 cloves garlic, peeled and crushed
1 green pepper, chopped
1 brinjal, cubed
1 tin (400 g) chopped, peeled tomatoes, drained
45 ml (3 tbsp) chopped fresh parsley
15 ml (1 tbsp) chopped fresh oregano or 5 ml (1 tsp) dried oregano
a pinch of sugar
4 x 100 g hake fillets
salt and milled black pepper

Preheat oven to 160 °C. Dry-fry onions and garlic in a saucepan *(see page xi)*, using stock to moisten. When onions are soft and golden, add green pepper and brinjal. Reduce heat and cook for 10 minutes, stirring occasionally. Add tomatoes, parsley, oregano and sugar. Season to taste. Simmer gently for 20 minutes, or until sauce is reduced and slightly thickened. Arrange hake in a single layer in a large ovenproof dish. Season with salt and pepper. Pour sauce evenly over hake fillets and bake, uncovered, for 35 minutes, or until fish is opaque and flakes easily. Serve with Greek rice.

Serves 4

COOK'S TIPS

x *Frozen hake fillets work well in this dish. If you're in a hurry, you needn't even defrost the fillets, but be sure to adjust the cooking time accordingly.*

devilled crab

An interesting way to prepare crab. Your friends will be amazed to find out how stunning crab can be.

625 ml (2$^1/_2$ cups) cooked crab meat
1 onion, finely chopped
1 green pepper, finely chopped
125 ml ($^1/_2$ cup) Kellogg's Cornflakes Crumbs
125 ml ($^1/_2$ cup) fat-free plain yoghurt
15 ml (1 tbsp) Dijon mustard
5 ml (1 tsp) Worcestershire sauce
30 ml (2 tbsp) brandy
30 ml (2 tbsp) chopped fresh parsley
2 ml ($^1/_2$ tsp) salt
2 ml ($^1/_2$ tsp) milled black pepper
2 ml ($^1/_2$ tsp) cayenne pepper
5 ml (1 tsp) Tabasco sauce, or to taste

TOPPING
80 ml ($^1/_3$ cup) Kellogg's Cornflakes Crumbs

Preheat oven to 220 °C. Shred crab meat and place in a mixing bowl. Add all remaining ingredients except topping and mix gently but thoroughly. Taste mixture and add more Tabasco and cayenne pepper if you prefer a hotter sauce. Pile mixture into a non-stick ovenproof baking dish, and top with crumbs. Bake uncovered for 15 minutes, or until golden brown and bubbling. Serve with Garlic Bread *(see page 5)* and a crisp green salad.

Serves 4

SEXY OPTIONS

For a really impressive appearance, Bake and serve the devilled crab in individual scallop shells.

fish in piquant tomato sauce

A quick one-dish meal that takes only a few minutes to prepare.

4 x 100 g firm white fish fillets
1 tin (400 g) tomato and onion mix
15 ml (1 tbsp) soft brown sugar
2 ribs celery, trimmed and finely sliced
30 ml (2 tbsp) capers, drained
2 ml (1/2 tsp) ground cumin
5 ml (1 tsp) ground coriander
juice of 1/2 lemon
5 ml (1 tsp) balsamic vinegar
salt and milled black pepper

Preheat oven to 220 °C. Arrange fish fillets in a single layer in a non-stick ovenproof dish. Combine all remaining ingredients and mix well. Pour sauce over fish and turn each fillet to ensure it is evenly coated. Place in a very hot oven and bake uncovered until fish is opaque and flakes easily (8–12 minutes, depending on the thickness of the fillets). Serve immediately with boiled new potatoes and Lemon Garlic Green Beans (see page 34).

Serves 4

SEXY OPTIONS

For an extra-lemony sauce, stir in the finely grated zest of 1 lemon. A handful of chopped fresh basil, parsley or oregano will add a Mediterranean flavour.

For a sauce with a real kick, de-seed and finely chop 1–2 fresh green chillies and sprinkle over fish before baking.

orange foil-baked haddock

This method of cooking keeps in all the juices and flavours and ensures that the fish remains moist and succulent.

4 x 100 g haddock loins
60 ml (1/4 cup) wholegrain mustard
60 ml (1/4 cup) tomato purée
60 ml (1/4 cup) dry vermouth
60 ml (1/4 cup) boiling water
5 ml (1 tsp) vegetable stock powder
juice of 1 lemon
juice of 3 oranges
salt and milled black pepper
mashed potato or Parsnip Purée (see page 28), to serve
finely chopped fresh parsley

Preheat oven to 220 °C. Place a non-stick baking sheet in the oven to heat up. Place a large double piece of tin foil, shiny side up, on your work surface. Arrange haddock loins in the centre of the foil, skin side down. Combine all remaining ingredients in a jug and whisk well. Drizzle sauce evenly over haddock fillets. Bring edges of foil together over the fish to form a roomy parcel, crimping edges to ensure that the juices won't leak out. Slide the parcel onto the heated baking tray and bake for 10–15 minutes. When fish is done, slit open the parcel and slide contents onto a warmed serving platter. Pipe a double edging of hot mashed potato or Parsnip Purée down either side of the platter. Sprinkle with chopped parsley and serve hot.

Serves 4

SEXY OPTIONS

For an Oriental flavour, add 10 ml (2 tsp) grated fresh ginger and some very finely sliced spring onions or lemon grass to the sauce. A generous pinch of Chinese five-spice powder imparts a fragrant note.

SEAFOOD & FISH

haddock paella

(See opposite)

A quick and easy treat that the whole family will enjoy. Not only does it taste good, it's a real feast for the eyes, with the bright yellow and green of the fish and vegetables.

1 large onion, finely chopped
1 green pepper, finely chopped
2 cloves garlic, peeled and crushed
1 tin (220 g) mussels in brine
750 ml–1 l (3–4 cups) hot water
500 ml (2 cups) long-grain rice
2 tomatoes, peeled and chopped
250 ml (1 cup) frozen peas
5 ml (1 tsp) turmeric
4 x 100 g haddock loins, poached and flaked (see Very Simple Haddock, page 53)
salt and milled black pepper
125 ml ($1/2$ cup) chopped fresh parsley

Dry-fry onion, green pepper and garlic (*see page xi*). Drain mussels well and reserve brine. Pour brine into a measuring jug and add enough water to make up 1 l (4 cups). When onion is softened and golden, pour in water/brine mixture. Add rice and tomatoes. Reduce heat, cover and simmer for 15 minutes. Add peas and turmeric, cover again and simmer until all the liquid has been absorbed and the rice is fluffy and soft. Fold in flaked haddock and reserved mussels, heat through for 2 minutes and remove from heat. Season with salt and milled black pepper. Serve hot, scattered with parsley and extra grindings of black pepper.

Serves 4–6

creamy herb kingklip

This is a quick, tasty dish that my guests ask for time and again. With its creamy, herby sauce and lovely colour, it's the perfect dish for a summer's evening.

1 onion, finely chopped
1 l (4 cups) fat-free milk
4 x 100 g kingklip fillets
125 ml ($1/2$ cup) finely shredded fresh basil leaves
125 ml ($1/2$ cup) finely chopped fresh parsley
30 ml (2 tbsp) cornflour
15 ml (1 tbsp) cake flour
salt and milled black pepper

Dry-fry onion in a large frying pan (*see page xi*). When onion is soft and transparent, pour in 875 ml ($3 1/2$ cups) of the milk. Heat to just below boiling point. Place kingklip fillets in milk, reduce heat and poach fillets very gently until just cooked (about 6–10 minutes, until the fish turns opaque and flakes easily). Using a slotted spoon, remove fish and arrange on a warmed platter. Add basil and parsley to hot milk. In a jug, mix cornflour, cake flour and remaining 125 ml ($1/2$ cup) milk to a smooth paste. Whisk paste into hot milk and cook over a low heat, stirring constantly to prevent lumps forming, until smooth and thickened. Pour sauce over fish fillets. Season with salt and pepper. Serve with boiled baby potatoes and peas.

Serves 4

SEXY OPTIONS

Real saffron will add luxurious colour and flavour to this paella. Soak the saffron filaments in 30 ml (2 tbsp) hot water and then add the saffron and the soaking water to the paella instead of the turmeric.

SEXY OPTIONS

To add extra flavour to the sauce, add a bay leaf, a few peppercorns, a stalk of parsley and a blade of mace to the poaching liquid. Remove flavourings before thickening.

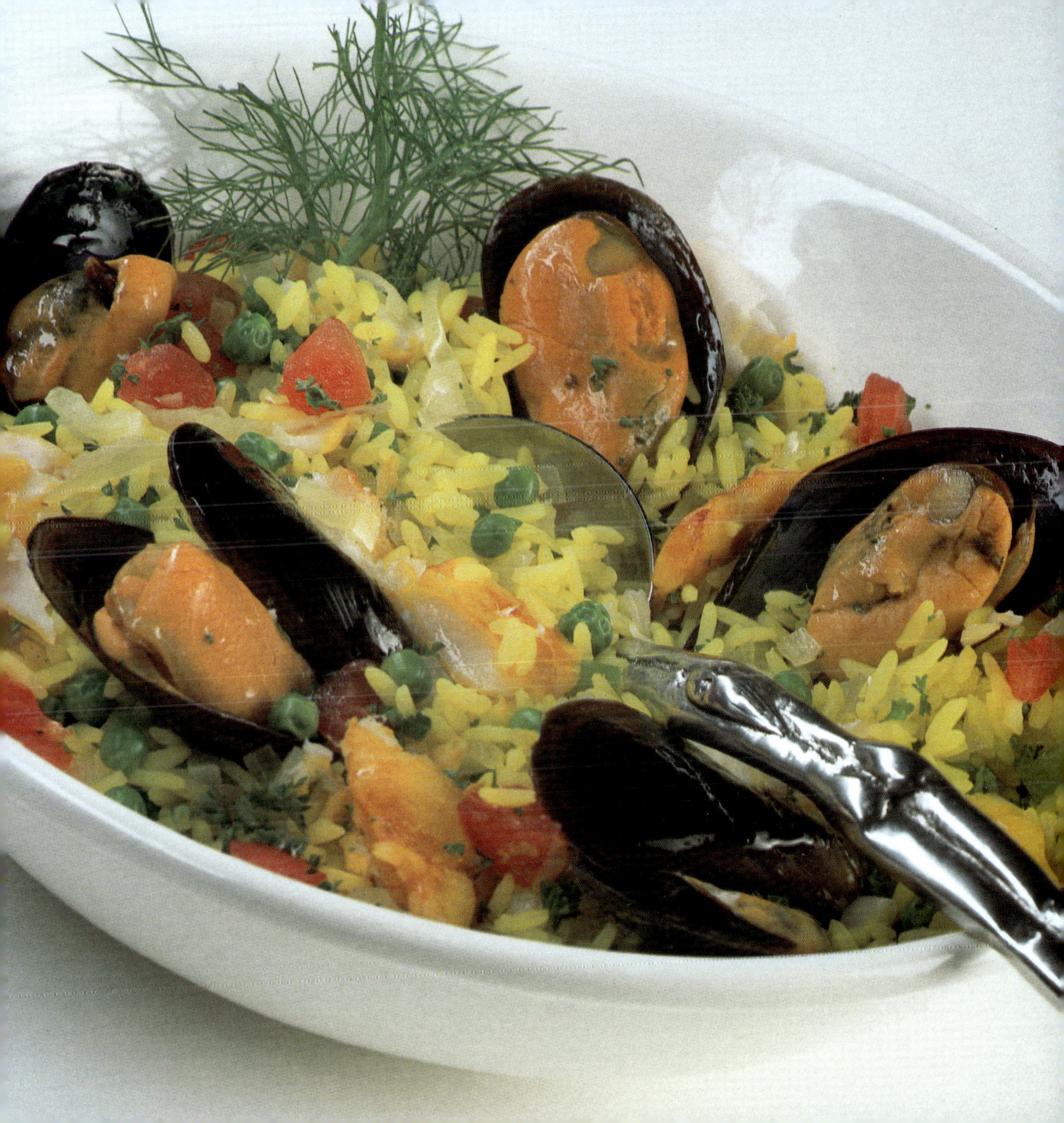

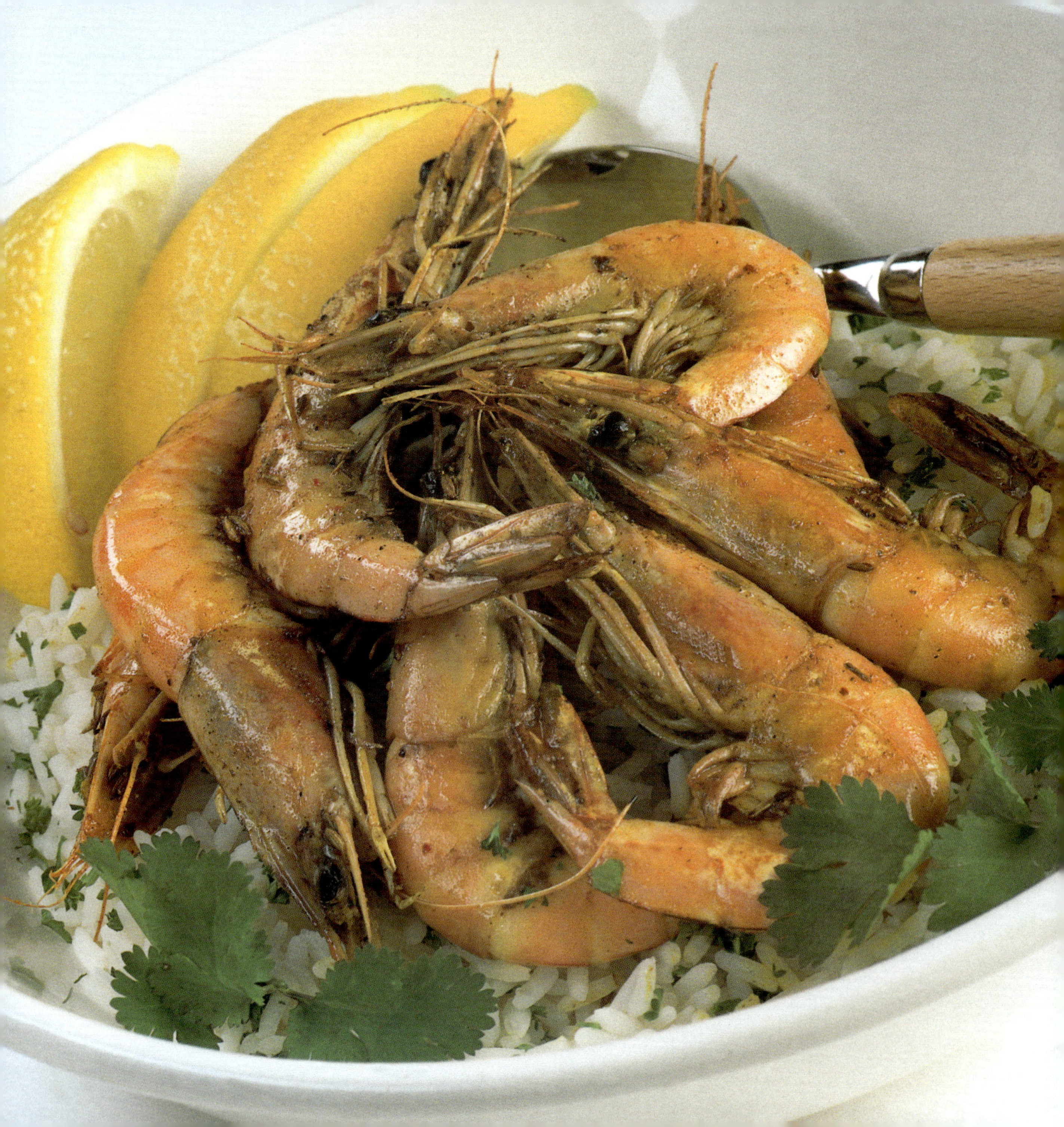

prawns madagascar

(See opposite)
With its subtle blend of spices, this finger-licking dish is ideal for a festive dinner party. Serve with a crisp white wine, Garlic Bread (see page 5) and a huge green salad.

125 ml (1/2 cup) water
125 ml (1/2 cup) red wine
24 large cooked prawns
salt and milled black pepper
chopped fresh coriander
lemon wedges

MADAGASCAR SPICE MIX
15 ml (1 tbsp) cumin seeds
15 ml (1 tbsp) coriander seeds
2 cardamom pods
10 ml (2 tsp) chilli powder or cayenne pepper, or to taste
15 ml (1 tbsp) turmeric
15 ml (1 tbsp) ground ginger
5 ml (1 tsp) ground cloves
a generous pinch of cinnamon

First make spice mix. Put cumin seeds, coriander seeds and cardamom pods in a hot, dry frying pan and heat for 1 minute, tossing constantly, until spices begin to crackle and release their aromas. Remove from pan and grind in a mortar and pestle. Remove cardamom husks and tip spices into a screw-top jar. Add chilli powder or cayenne pepper, turmeric, ginger, cloves and cinnamon. Screw on lid and shake very well to combine. Reserve. Heat a heavy-bottomed frying pan and add a teaspoon or two of water. Add 15 ml (1 tbsp) of the spice mix and 'fry' the mixture for about 30 seconds. Remove pan from heat and add half the water and half the wine. Put in half the prawns, return to the heat and toss well to ensure that prawns are well coated with spices. Cook for about 1 minute on each side, then remove with a slotted spoon, put on a warmed platter, cover and keep warm. Add remaining wine, water and prawns to pan and repeat procedure. Remove with a slotted spoon. Put remaining spice mix in pan, to taste. Season with salt and pepper. Cook sauce until slightly reduced. Arrange prawns on a bed of hot rice and pour over sauce. Garnish with chopped coriander and lemon wedges and serve hot.

Serves 4

COOK'S TIPS

x If you are in too much of a hurry to grind your own spices, use ready-ground ones. Ensure, however, that they are very fresh, as the success of this dish depends on how aromatic the spices are.

x Store any leftover Madagascar spice mix in a tightly sealed jar in a dark cupboard. Use for coating fish or skinned, deboned chicken breasts.

luxury oven-poached sole

I'm very fond of sole, with its tender, delicate flesh, and this is a lovely way to prepare it. Fresh sole is best, but if you can't find it, use a good quality frozen brand.

80 ml (2/3 cup) dry vermouth
60 ml (1/4 cup) chopped fresh parsley
juice of 1 lemon
4 whole sole, skinned
salt and milled black pepper

Preheat oven to 220 °C. Combine vermouth, parsley and lemon juice in a jug. Pour a third of this mixture into a non-stick, ovenproof dish big enough to hold all the fish in one layer. Arrange sole in the dish. Season generously with salt and pepper and pour over remaining liquid. Bake uncovered for 7–10 minutes, or until fish is opaque and flakes easily. Remove with a slotted spoon, drain well and arrange on a warmed platter. Garnish with lemon wedges and sprigs of parsley. Serve with Broccoli Gratin (see page 32).

SEAFOOD & FISH

three-pepper and tuna bake

This colourful dish will be appreciated by those who prefer a less 'fishy' flavour.

2 onions, finely chopped
2 small leeks, trimmed and finely sliced
1 red pepper, finely sliced
1 green pepper, finely sliced
1 yellow pepper, finely sliced
45 ml (3 tbsp) cornflour
500 ml (2 cups) fat-free milk
2 tins (200 g each) tuna in brine, drained and flaked
10 ml (2 tsp) dried mixed Italian herbs
salt and milled black pepper

TOPPING
2 tomatoes, sliced
125 ml (1/2 cup) Kellogg's Cornflakes Crumbs
5 ml (1 tsp) sugar
10 ml (2 tsp) chopped fresh parsley

Preheat oven to 180 °C. Dry-fry onions and leeks (see page xi). When onions and leeks are golden brown, add red, green and yellow peppers and continue dry-frying until peppers are soft. In a teacup, mix cornflour with enough of the milk to form a smooth, runny paste. Stir paste into onions and peppers along with remaining milk. Cook over a low heat, stirring constantly, until sauce is thick and smooth. Add tuna and dried herbs and season with salt and pepper. Tip mixture into a non-stick ovenproof dish and top with slices of tomato. Sprinkle over crumbs, sugar and parsley. Bake for 20 minutes, or until top is golden brown. Serve with sweetcorn kernels and a crisp green salad.

Serves 4

prawn risotto

The secret to a good risotto is to watch it like a hawk, and to add the liquid little by little to result in a thick, creamy mixture.

1 onion, very finely chopped
375 ml (1 1/2 cups) risotto rice (see Cook's tips)
stock made with 1.25 l (5 cups) boiling water and 20 ml (4 tsp) stock powder
500 ml (2 cups) small raw shelled prawns
salt and milled black pepper
45 ml (3 tbsp) chopped fresh parsley

Gently dry-fry onion in a large saucepan (see page xi). When onion is soft and transparent (do not allow to brown) add rice and 30 ml (2 tbsp) stock. Cook rice, stirring constantly, until lightly toasted. When all the liquid has been absorbed, add a little more stock. Continue adding hot stock, a little at a time, stirring gently. Allow the stock to be completely absorbed before you add any more. When you have used up half the stock, add prawns. Continue adding stock, stirring gently all the time, until rice is cooked and creamy but still al dente (with a little bite). This should take about 20 minutes. Remove from heat and stir in salt, pepper and parsley. Leave to stand for 3 minutes, and serve hot.

Serves 4

COOK'S TIPS

x For a classic, creamy risotto, you will need to use Italian arborio rice (available from most good supermarkets). You can use long-grain white rice, but the result will be fluffier and drier.

x For a more delicate flavour, use finely sliced spring onions in place of onions.

curried crayfish

Crayfish is too pricey to serve every day, but a little does go a long way. This mildly spicy curried dish is ideal for an informal dinner party. Serve with boiled rice and a crisp white wine.

Need stock

2 cooked crayfish
1 large onion, chopped
1 clove garlic, peeled and crushed
15 ml (1 tbsp) mild curry powder
5 ml (1 tsp) lemon juice
10 ml (2 tsp) tomato paste
stock made with 250 ml (1 cup) boiling water and 5 ml
    (1 tsp) fish stock powder
60 ml (¼ cup) white wine
15 ml (1 tbsp) cake flour
15 ml (1 tbsp) water
2 tomatoes, peeled, de-seeded and chopped
1 green apple, cored, peeled and grated
15 ml (1 tbsp) apricot jam
salt and milled black pepper

Using the tip of a sharp knife, split crayfish along the centre. Remove the black thread from the tail and the sac from below the head. Remove flesh and cut into pieces. Crack claws, remove flesh and reserve. Dry-fry onion and garlic (*see page xi*). When onion is softened, add curry powder and cook for 1 minute to release the aroma. Add lemon juice, tomato paste, stock and wine. Put flour in a teacup, add the water and mix to a smooth paste. Whisk paste into hot sauce and cook over a low heat, stirring constantly, until sauce is smooth and thick. Add tomatoes, apple and apricot jam. Reduce heat, cover and simmer for 15 minutes. Stir in reserved crayfish meat and heat through. Season with salt and pepper. Serve on a bed of boiled rice.

Serves 4

COOK'S TIPS

x *If you can't find whole crayfish, use frozen crayfish tails. Remember to defrost before cooking.*

x *Cooked prawns may be substituted for crayfish.*

grilled fish with spiced yoghurt

This unusual recipe is the one to try when you're bored with traditional fish dishes. Any firm white fish fillet can be used, including hake, kingklip and kabeljou.

250 ml (1 cup) fat-free milk
4 x 100 g firm white fish fillets
5 ml (1 tsp) ground cumin
5 ml (1 tsp) ground coriander
5 ml (1 tsp) ground cardamom
30 ml (2 tbsp) sherry
30 ml (2 tbsp) lemon juice
250 ml (1 cup) fat-free plain yoghurt
salt and milled black pepper

Preheat grill to its hottest setting. Heat milk in a saucepan to just below boiling point and put in the fish fillets. Poach fish very briefly (about 1–2 minutes on each side). Remove with a slotted spoon, drain well and arrange in a single layer in a non-stick ovenproof dish. Put cumin, coriander and cardamom in a dry frying pan and heat until they begin to crackle and smell aromatic. Add sherry and stir well. Remove from heat and stir in lemon juice and yoghurt. Season with salt and pepper. Spoon this mixture evenly over fish fillets and place under grill. Grill for 3–5 minutes, or until fish is cooked through. Serve hot on a bed of turmeric rice *(see Sexy options, page 47)* with wedges of lemon and Baby Marrows Provençal *(see page 34)*.

Serves 4

SEAFOOD & FISH

carefree paella

I gave this dish its name because it has all the flavour and colour of a traditional Spanish paella but none of the fat.

1 large onion, finely sliced
2 cloves garlic, peeled and crushed
1 red pepper, finely chopped
125 ml ($^1/_2$ cup) white wine
2 tomatoes, peeled and chopped
375 ml (1$^1/_2$ cups) long-grain rice
stock made with 625 ml (2$^1/_2$ cups) boiling water and 5 ml (1 tsp) chicken stock powder
5 ml (1 tsp) turmeric
8–10 cooked, shelled prawns
1 cooked crayfish tail, flesh removed and diced
12 cooked mussels in their shells
12 frozen smoked oysters (see Cook's tips)
250 ml (1 cup) frozen peas
salt and milled black pepper
chopped fresh parsley

Dry-fry onion, garlic and red pepper in a large saucepan, using the wine to moisten (see page xi). When onion is soft and golden, add tomatoes, rice and stock and simmer, covered, for 5 minutes. Stir in turmeric. Arrange prawns, crayfish meat, mussels, oysters and peas on top of the rice. Cover again and simmer gently for 15–20 minutes, or until rice is cooked and fluffy and most of the liquid has been absorbed. Season with salt and pepper. Scatter with chopped fresh parsley and serve immediately.

Serves 4

COOK'S TIPS

x Frozen smoked oysters are stocked by good fishmongers. If you can't find them, use baby calamari tubes instead, but remember to add them to the paella just a few minutes before serving to prevent them toughening.

foil-wrapped spaghetti with shellfish

This is a fun way to serve shellfish at an informal dinner party, and you don't have to spend a fortune on expensive ingredients.

12 clams in their shells
12 mussels in their shells
12 small cooked shelled prawns
3 tomatoes, peeled
stock made with 250 ml (1 cup) boiling water and 5 ml (1 tsp) vegetable stock powder
2 cloves garlic, peeled and crushed
5–10 ml (1–2 tsp) cayenne pepper, to taste
15 ml (1 tbsp) chopped fresh parsley
10 fresh basil leaves, torn into small pieces
500 g spaghetti
salt and milled black pepper

Preheat oven to 220 °C. Clean clams and mussels thoroughly to remove all traces of grit (see Cook's tips, page 50). Rinse prawns under running water. Put tomatoes in a blender or food processor and liquidise to a pulp. Reserve. Heat half the stock in a saucepan. Add garlic and cayenne pepper. Put in all the shellfish, bring to the boil and cook briskly for 2 minutes, adding a little more stock if the pan dries out, and stirring gently all the time. Stir in tomato pulp, parsley, basil and any remaining stock. Reduce heat, cover and simmer for 5 minutes. Meanwhile, cook the spaghetti for just 6–7 minutes (it should only be half-cooked). Drain quickly in a colander and return to cooking pot. Pour seafood sauce over spaghetti and mix gently but thoroughly. Season with salt and black pepper. Line a baking sheet with a double layer of tin foil, shiny side up. Turn up the edges all the way round to prevent juices from escaping. Turn spaghetti and seafood mixture onto foil and quickly bring up long edges to form a long cylindrical parcel. Seal tightly. Bake for 10 minutes. Transfer parcel to a heated serving platter (use two spatulas) and open at the table.

Serves 4

kingklip with mediterranean salsa

It's essential to use fresh herbs in the salsa for that authentic Mediterranean flavour. Serve with plenty of crusty Italian bread for mopping up the juices.

4 x 100 g fresh kingklip fillets or any other firm white fish
stock made with 250 ml (1 cup) boiling water, 250 ml (1 cup) white wine and 10 ml (2 tsp) vegetable stock powder
1 onion, quartered
1 large carrot, peeled and finely sliced
1 bay leaf
1 sprig fresh parsley
1 sprig fresh thyme
2 slices lemon

MEDITERRANEAN SALSA
3 ripe tomatoes, peeled, de-seeded and chopped
1 onion, finely chopped
2 cloves garlic, peeled and crushed
15 ml (1 tbsp) chopped fresh oregano
15 ml (1 tbsp) fresh basil leaves, torn into pieces
15 ml (1 tbsp) chopped fresh parsley
5 ml (1 tsp) paprika or chilli powder
5 ml (1 tsp) red or white wine vinegar
3 jalapeño peppers, de-seeded and very finely chopped, or to taste (see Cook's tips)
salt and pepper

Arrange fish in a single layer in a large lidded frying pan. Pour over hot stock and add onion, carrot, bay leaf, parsley, thyme and lemon slices. Bring stock up to simmering point, cover and poach fish gently for 10 minutes, or until flesh is opaque and flakes easily. Use a slotted spoon to transfer fish to a warmed platter and keep warm. Strain poaching liquid and reserve. To make the salsa, combine all ingredients in a bowl and mix gently. Stir in 250 ml (1 cup) of the reserved poaching liquid while it is still warm. Season with salt and pepper. Pour salsa over fish and serve immediately.

Serves 4

COOK'S TIPS

x If you're in a hurry, put salsa ingredients into the goblet of a food processor and blend briefly to form a chunky sauce.

x Jalapeño peppers have a mild flavour that is well suited to this salsa. If you can't find them, use a fresh green chilli instead.

x If this salsa seems all together too fiery for your tastes, simmer it gently for 10 minutes to mellow the flavours.

kingklip magic

This dish truly earns its name – it's quick and easy to cook, it's always popular with guests and it tastes, well, like magic.

4 x 100 g fresh kingklip fillets
80 ml (1/3 cup) lemon juice
30 ml (2 tbsp) soy sauce
15 ml (1 tbsp) chopped fresh oregano
1 clove garlic, peeled and crushed
salt and milled black pepper

Preheat grill to its hottest setting. Put fish in a single layer in a shallow ovenproof dish. Combine lemon juice, soy sauce, oregano and garlic and season to taste with salt and black pepper. Drizzle half this mixture evenly over fish fillets. Place fillets as close to grill as possible and grill for about 5 minutes, depending on thickness of fish. Turn fillets over with a pair of tongs, drizzle with remaining basting liquid and grill for a further 3–5 minutes, until fish is cooked through. Serve with new potatoes and a green salad or Braised Fennel with Tomato (see page 32).

Serves 4

sole with spinach and scallop sauce

A light and pretty dish perfect for a winter's evening. Serve with a bottle of good Chardonnay.

4 whole sole, skinned
60 ml ($^1/_2$ cup) lemon juice
5 ml (1 tsp) salt
5 ml (1 tsp) milled black pepper

SAUCE
1 bunch spinach
6 slim leeks, trimmed
80 ml ($^1/_3$ cup) dry white wine
60 ml ($^1/_4$ cup) dry vermouth
12 scallops (see Cook's tips)
15 ml (1 tbsp) cornflour
80 ml ($^1/_3$ cup) fat-free plain yoghurt
15 ml (1 tbsp) chopped fresh parsley

Preheat oven to 160 °C. To make the sauce, pull stalks and any tough strands off spinach leaves and rinse well to remove all traces of grit. Place wet spinach in a large pot over a medium heat (there will be enough water clinging to the leaves to cook the spinach). Cover with a lid and cook, stirring and turning spinach occasionally, for 10–15 minutes, or until well wilted. Drain thoroughly in a colander, using a plate to press out excess moisture. Tip onto a board and chop finely. Reserve. Place sole on a large double piece of tin foil, shiny side up, and sprinkle with lemon juice. Season with salt and pepper and wrap to form a tight parcel. Place parcel on a baking sheet and bake for 15 minutes. Meanwhile, cut leeks into long, thin strips. Dry-fry leeks (see page xi). When leeks are soft and golden, add wine and vermouth. Reduce heat, add scallops and simmer for 1 minute. Remove pan from heat. Mix cornflour with enough yoghurt to make a smooth paste. Add paste to sauce along with remaining yoghurt, parsley and reserved spinach. Cook over a low heat, stirring constantly, until sauce is smooth and thick. Season with salt and pepper. Remove sole from oven, slit foil package and slide fish onto a heated platter. Pour over sauce. Serve hot with new potatoes and Glazed Baby Carrots (see page 33).

Serves 4

SEXY OPTIONS

This is a lovely dinner party dish. Ask your fishmonger to fillet the sole for you, and to roll each fillet. Allow 2–4 rolled fillets per person.

Garnish the dish with tiny peeled baby shrimps and a feathery frond of dill or fennel.

COOK'S TIPS

x *Tinned or frozen scallops may be used. If you can't find either and are in the mood for splashing out, use 12 fresh oysters.*

x *If you're in a hurry, use frozen spinach instead of fresh, but be sure to drain it very thoroughly after cooking to prevent it from diluting the sauce.*

chicken

On the X Diet, chicken breast fillets are a delicious way to keep the fat low and the flavours high. Simple chicken breasts are fairly delicate with their flavour, so we have developed several ways of cooking them, getting inspiration from many household favourites and cultural variations. It is imperative that we move well away from the plain, poached or grilled methods of preparation, because these are too embroiled in the diet mentality and the flavours and textures do not do justice to the best part of chicken.

As always, sauces are tops and, by using the ever-present dry-fry method, you can enjoy plenty of rich and indulgent dishes with your family, and have them coming back for seconds and thirds!

spiced yoghurt chicken

This is my family's all-time favourite chicken dish. It's quick to make and has a delicious 'kick'. Serve with plenty of basmati rice and a crisp green salad.

4 skinned, deboned chicken breasts, cut into thin strips
5 ml (1 tsp) ground cumin
5 ml (1 tsp) ground coriander
juice of 1/2 lemon
500 ml (2 cups) fat-free plain yoghurt
80 ml (1/3 cup) chopped fresh parsley
salt and milled black pepper

Preheat oven to 180 °C. Dry-fry chicken strips over a high heat (see page xi). Add cumin, coriander and lemon juice. Continue dry-frying until spices are browned and chicken is cooked through (about 20 seconds). Reduce heat and stir in yoghurt and parsley. Season generously with salt and pepper. Gently warm through for 3 minutes (no longer, or the yoghurt may curdle). Serve with lemon wedges, basmati rice and a green salad.

Serves 4

COOK'S TIPS

x For a spicier sauce, add 5 ml (1 tsp) cayenne pepper. A pinch of turmeric will give the chicken a lovely warm yellow colour.

x Don't cook the chicken for any longer than 3 minutes after you have added the yoghurt, as the yoghurt is inclined to curdle at high temperatures. You can stabilise the yoghurt first by beating in 10 ml (2 tsp) cornflour.

x If you have the time, marinate the chicken in the lemon juice and spices for a few hours before cooking.

quick chicken curry

This 'idiot's version' of chicken curry is by no means an authentic dish, but one designed for the person who is always on the run. The cola is an unusual ingredient but it makes the chicken deliciously sticky and brown.

1 onion, finely chopped
30 ml (2 tbsp) medium curry powder
4 skinned, deboned chicken breasts, cut into thin strips
125 ml (1/2 cup) Coca-Cola
500 ml (2 cups) fat-free plain yoghurt or buttermilk
salt and milled black pepper

SAMBALS
finely chopped onion and tomato
chopped fresh coriander
Tzatziki (see page 4)
fruity chutney
sliced banana tossed in lemon juice

Dry-fry onions (see page xi). When onions are softened and brown, add curry powder. Toss over a high heat until curry powder begins to stick. Add chicken and a little Coca-Cola. Dry-fry chicken, adding remaining Coca-Cola until strips are brown and cooked through (about 20 seconds). Reduce heat and stir in yoghurt or buttermilk. Season generously with salt and pepper. Warm through for 3 minutes (no longer, or the yoghurt may curdle). Serve with basmati rice and pass around the sambals in separate bowls.

Serves 4

creamy chicken and brinjal curry

This mild curry has such a creamy sauce that it's difficult to believe it doesn't contain a litre of fresh cream! Somehow, the combination of brinjal, yoghurt and evaporated milk conspires to create an unctuous texture that is quite irresistible.

3 onions, chopped
2 large brinjals, diced
1 tin (400 g) tomato and onion mix
4 skinned, deboned chicken breasts, cubed
125 ml (½ cup) fat-free milk
250 ml (1 cup) fat-free plain yoghurt
30 ml (2 tbsp) grated fresh ginger
4 cloves garlic, peeled and crushed
1 bunch fresh coriander
15 ml (1 tbsp) cornflour
2–3 fresh green chillies, de-seeded, to taste
salt and milled black pepper

SPICE MIXTURE
5 ml (1 tsp) coriander seeds, dry-roasted and ground (see page xiii)
5 ml (1 tsp) cumin seeds, dry-roasted and ground
2 ml (½ tsp) cardamom pods, dry-roasted and ground
5 ml (1 tsp) mild curry powder
5 ml (1 tsp) turmeric

TOPPING
5 ml (1 tsp) mustard seeds
chopped fresh coriander

First make the spice mixture. Heat a dry frying pan and add coriander, cumin, cardamom, curry powder and turmeric. Toast the spices for 1 minute, or until they release their fragrance. Add onion and dry-fry (*see page xi*). When onions are soft and well browned, put in brinjal cubes. Cook over a high heat, tossing the brinjals until they brown. Add tomato and onion mix, reduce heat and simmer for 10 minutes. Add chicken and simmer very gently until chicken pieces are just cooked (about 7 minutes). Meanwhile, put milk, yoghurt, ginger, garlic, fresh coriander, cornflour and chillies into a food processor or blender. Blend to a fine, creamy paste. Add the yoghurt paste to the chicken a few tablespoons at a time, stirring constantly between each addition. When all the yoghurt paste has been added, simmer curry for another 10 minutes, until thickened and creamy. Season with salt and black pepper. Put mustard seeds in a dry frying pan and heat until they begin to crackle and pop. Sprinkle curry with mustard seeds and more fresh coriander. Serve immediately with basmati rice and a fruity chutney.

Serves 4

COOK'S TIPS

x *Be sure to add the yoghurt paste to the hot sauce gradually, a few tablespoons at a time, as this — along with the cornflour — prevents the sauce from curdling.*

x *Make an extra-large supply of spice mixture and keep it in an airtight container for the next curry you make.*

thai chicken kebabs

Anyone who feels they can't face another braai with burnt boerewors and greasy chops will appreciate these succulent Thai-style kebabs.

4 skinned, deboned chicken breasts
1 red pepper
1 yellow pepper
500 ml (2 cups) mange-touts or sugarsnap peas
8 pickled jalapeño peppers, optional
8 cooked, shelled prawns
1 tin (400 g) litchis, plus their juice
fresh coriander sprigs

MARINADE
reserved juice from litchis
10 ml (2 tsp) coconut essence
45 ml (3 tbsp) lemon juice
10 ml (2 tsp) John West Thai Red Curry Paste
500 ml (2 cups) fat-free plain yoghurt
10 ml (2 tsp) ground ginger
a handful of chopped fresh coriander
salt and milled black pepper

Cut chicken and peppers into cubes of roughly the same size. Top and tail the mange-touts or sugarsnap peas and cut each one in half. If you're using jalapeño peppers, drain well and cut each one in half. Thread the pieces onto skewers in contrasting patterns. Arrange in a single layer in a shallow glass dish. To make marinade, combine all ingredients in a small jug and whisk well. Pour marinade over kebabs, cover with clingwrap and refrigerate for at least 3 hours, preferably overnight. Cook over medium coals, turning and basting frequently, until chicken is cooked through (20–30 minutes). Garnish with fresh coriander sprigs and serve with rice and a green salad.

Makes about 8 kebabs

COOK'S TIPS

x *Don't make the chicken cubes too large as they will burn on the outside before they cook on the inside. A cube of about 1.5 cm is ideal.*

chicken à la king

This fat-free version means you can still enjoy the original — without any guilt!

1 onion, chopped
4 skinned, deboned chicken breasts, cut into thin strips
2 green peppers, sliced into thin rings
1 punnet (about 300 g) button mushrooms, sliced
1 clove garlic, peeled and crushed
60 ml ($^1/_4$ cup) sherry
30 ml (2 tbsp) cornflour
45 ml (3 tbsp) fat-free milk powder
750 ml (3 cups) fat-free milk
500 ml (2 cups) frozen peas
10 ml (2 tsp) white sugar
salt and milled black pepper

Dry-fry onion, chicken, green peppers, mushrooms and garlic (*see page xi*). When onion is softened and golden brown, add sherry, reduce heat and simmer for about 10 minutes, or until peppers are soft and chicken is cooked through. Put cornflour and milk powder in a teacup and add enough of the milk to make a smooth, runny paste. Stir paste into chicken sauce along with remaining milk. Cook over a low heat, stirring constantly, until sauce is smooth and thick. Stir in peas and sugar and simmer until peas are just cooked (about 5 minutes; they should retain their bright green colour). Season generously with salt and pepper. Serve hot with rice.

Serves 4

smoked chicken and mushroom tagliolini

An unusual and beguiling flavour makes this dish ideal for serving to dinner-party guests. An added bonus is that it's very quick to make.

3 cloves garlic, peeled and crushed
6 slices shaved, smoked chicken, cut into squares
1 yellow pepper, cut into strips
1 green pepper, cut into strips
6 sun-dried tomatoes, chopped (see Cook's tips)
1 punnet (about 300 g) large brown mushrooms, sliced
5 ml (1 tsp) soy sauce
10 ml (2 tsp) tomato purée
a generous pinch of chilli flakes, to taste
80 ml ($1/3$ cup) dry vermouth
salt and milled black pepper
500 g tagliolini or tagliatelle

Dry-fry garlic, smoked chicken, yellow pepper and green pepper (see page xi). When peppers are soft, add sun-dried tomatoes, mushrooms, soy sauce, tomato purée and chilli flakes. Reduce heat and simmer, uncovered, for 10–15 minutes, or until the liquid is reduced to a few tablespoons. Meanwhile, cook tagliolini in plenty of boiling salted water. Drain in a colander, then tip into a deep warmed bowl. Add vermouth to vegetables in saucepan, season with salt and pepper and remove from the heat immediately. Pour sauce over hot pasta and mix together carefully. Serve with a spinach salad topped with Crunchy Croûtons (see page 12).

Serves 4

COOK'S TIPS

x Be sure to use sun-dried tomatoes from a packet, not those that are steeped in oil. If peppers aren't available, use 1 onion, finely chopped, and a few thinly sliced baby marrows.

golden chicken nuggets

A two-in-one recipe: these crunchy crumbed chicken pieces are accompanied by a spicy sweetcorn and rice casserole that goes in the oven at the same time. Just the dish for feeding a crowd of ravenous teenagers.

250–375 ml (1–1$1/2$ cups) Kellogg's Cornflakes Crumbs
250 ml (1 cup) fat-free plain yoghurt
10 ml (2 tsp) prepared English mustard
90 ml (6 tbsp) Worcestershire sauce
5 ml (1 tsp) salt
15 ml (1 tbsp) sugar
4 skinned, deboned chicken breasts, cut into 2 cm cubes

RICE CASSEROLE
500 ml (2 cups) cooked long-grain rice
250 ml (1 cup) frozen whole kernel sweetcorn
1 green pepper, finely chopped
1 red pepper, finely chopped
30 ml (2 tbsp) fruity chutney
salt and milled black pepper
15–30 ml (1–2 tbsp) paprika, for sprinkling
Tomato and Chilli Salsa (see page 6), to serve

Preheat oven to 180 °C. Put crumbs in a shallow dish. In a separate bowl, mix together yoghurt, mustard, Worcestershire sauce, salt and sugar. Add all the chicken cubes and mix well. Spear a chicken cube with a fork, shake off excess liquid and transfer to dish of crumbs. Toss cube in crumbs, making sure it is evenly coated. Place on a non-stick baking sheet. Repeat with remaining cubes. Refrigerate while you make the rice casserole. In a bowl, combine rice, sweetcorn, peppers, chutney, salt and pepper and any remaining yoghurt mixture. Mix thoroughly and tip into a small non-stick ovenproof dish. If the mixture seems too dry, add a little more yoghurt. Press down mixture with the back of a wooden spoon and sprinkle with paprika. Place chicken nuggets on top shelf of oven, put casserole, uncovered, on lower shelf and bake for 30 minutes, or until chicken is golden and cooked through. Serve hot with lemon wedges and Tomato and Chilli Salsa.

Serves 4

chicken and pineapple kebabs

(See opposite)

Next time you're invited to a braai, take along these tasty chicken kebabs. Chances are you'll have to share them, so make a double quantity. I've given two different marinades — take your pick, or invent your own!

KEBABS
4 skinned, deboned chicken breasts
2 green peppers
2 onions or 16 pickling onions
1 punnet (about 300 g) button mushrooms
1 tin (400 g) pineapple rings, drained

MARINADE 1
250 ml (1 cup) soy sauce
45 ml (3 tbsp) brown sugar
30 ml (2 tbsp) lemon juice
2 cloves garlic, peeled and crushed
30 ml (2 tbsp) grated fresh ginger
salt and milled black pepper

MARINADE 2
125 ml ($^1/_2$ cup) tomato sauce
60 ml ($^1/_4$ cup) white wine vinegar
30 ml (2 tbsp) brown sugar
7 ml (1 heaped tsp) prepared English mustard
salt and milled black pepper

Cut chicken, green peppers and onions into cubes of roughly the same size. If you're using pickling onions, peel them and leave them whole. Halve button mushrooms and cut each pineapple ring into 6 pieces. Thread the pieces onto skewers in contrasting patterns. Arrange in a single layer in a shallow glass dish. To make marinade, combine all ingredients for Marinade 1 or 2 in a small jug and whisk well. Pour marinade over kebabs, cover with clingwrap and refrigerate overnight. Cook over medium coals, turning and basting frequently, until chicken is cooked through (20–30 minutes). Serve with baked potatoes or Cheesy Stuffed Potatoes (*see page 31*) and a green salad.

Makes about 8 kebabs

SEXY OPTIONS

A fresh bay leaf threaded onto the pointed end of each skewer will produce a lovely aromatic smoke as the kebabs cook. Remove before serving.

Omit the soy sauce from Marinade 1 and add 250 ml (1 cup) white wine, the finely grated zest of 1 lemon and a handful of chopped fresh coriander or lemon grass.

Add 125 ml ($^1/_2$ cup) red wine, a large dollop of chutney and a dash of cayenne pepper to Marinade 2.

chilli chicken

A quick dish with a gentle kick. The bachelor with a penchant for chillies and no-fuss meals will appreciate this dish.

4 skinned, deboned chicken breasts, cubed
stock made with 125 ml ($^1/_2$ cup) boiling water and 5 ml (1 tsp) chicken stock powder
15 ml (1 tbsp) chilli flakes, or to taste
2 cloves garlic, peeled and crushed
1 tin (400 g) baked beans in tomato sauce

Dry-fry chicken (*see page xi*) until chicken sears and begins to stick to the bottom of the pan. Pour in stock and stir well. Add chilli flakes and garlic. Reduce heat, cover and simmer gently for 10–15 minutes, or until chicken pieces are cooked through. Add baked beans and mix well. Serve hot with brown rice and a green salad.

Serves 4

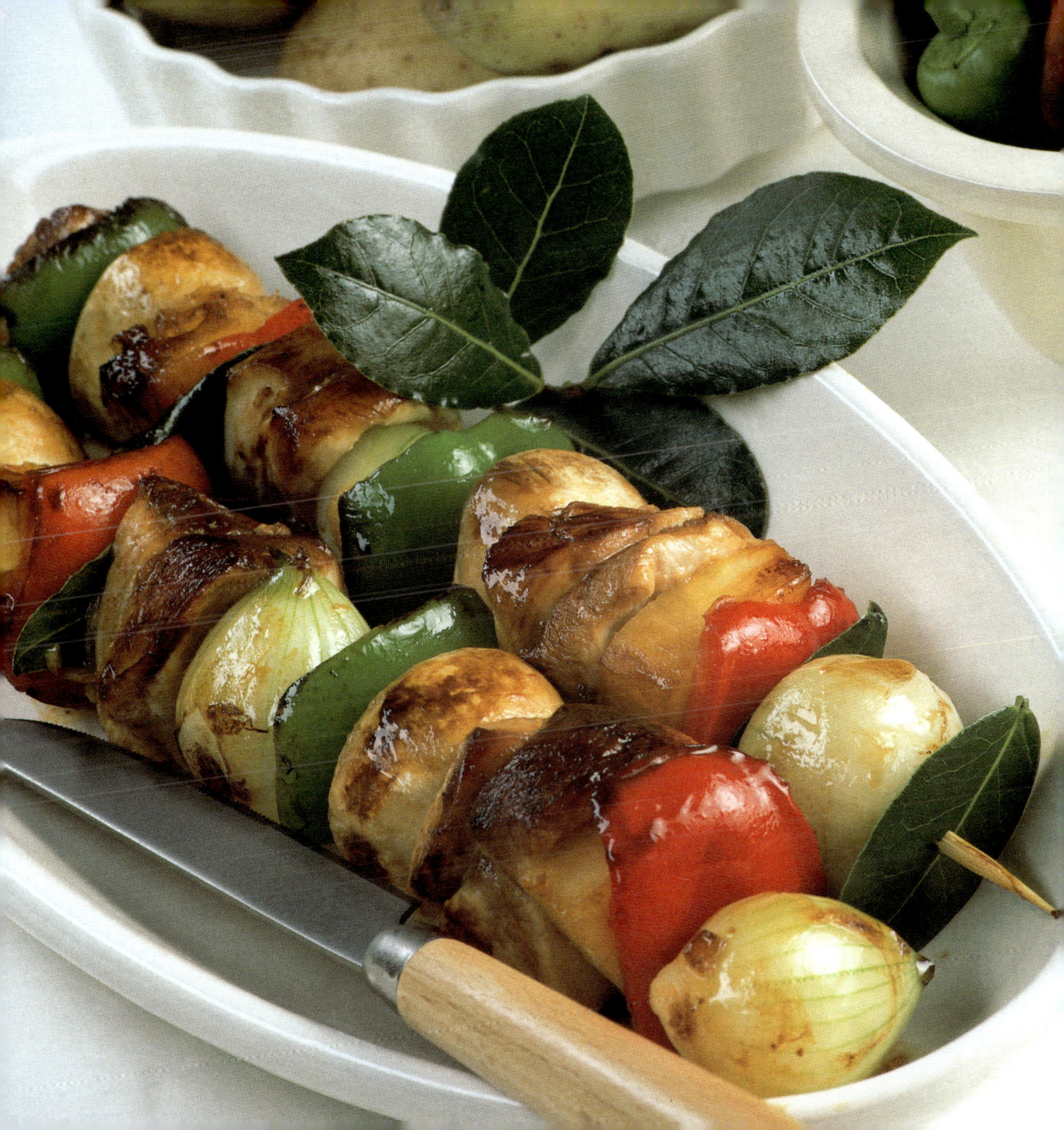

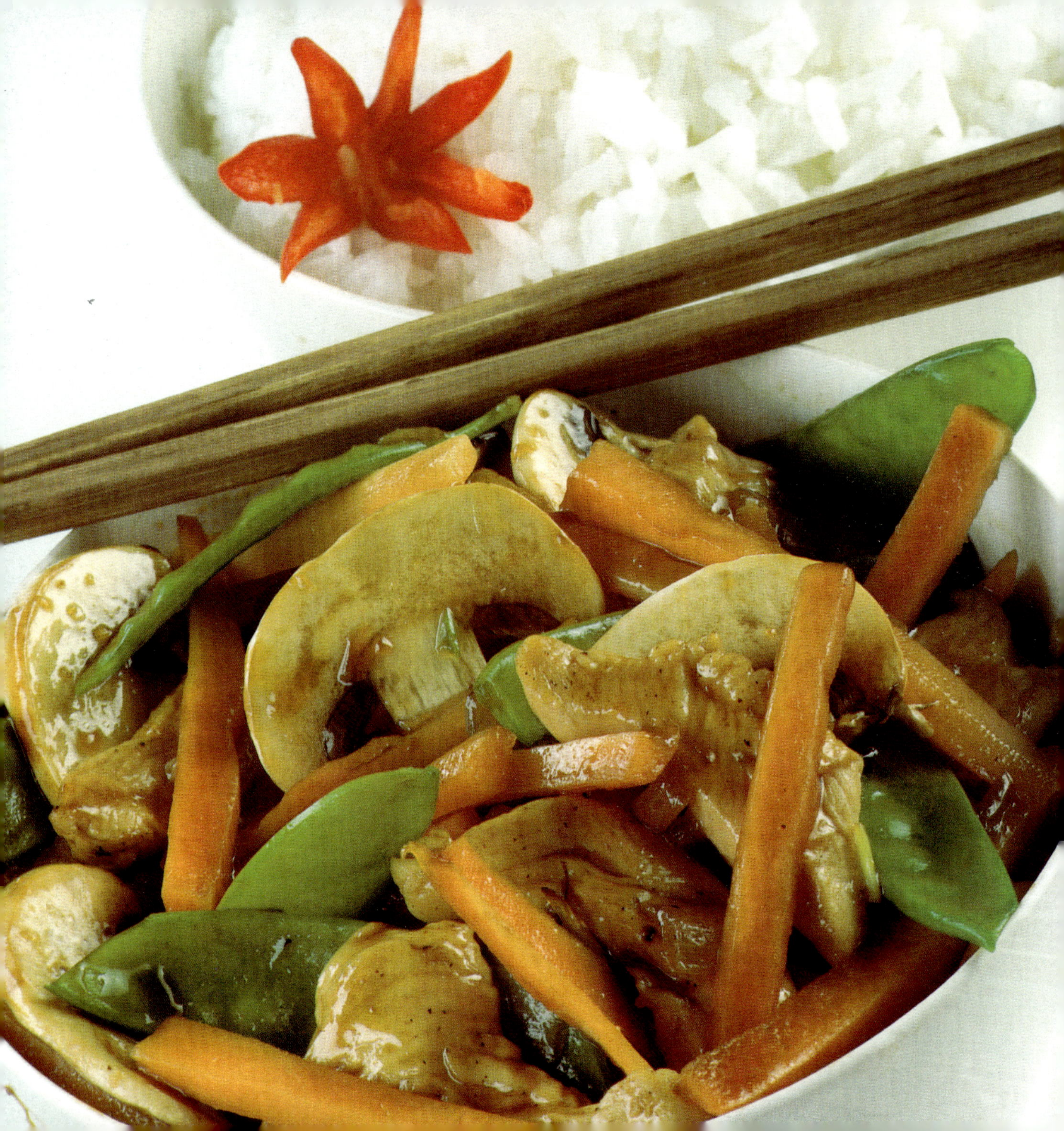

chinese chicken

(See opposite)

A delightful dinner party dish that I like to save for special occasions. Try to find jasmine rice (available from good supermarkets or Oriental stores) to serve with the chicken, and use a thick, dark soy sauce, as the sauce needs to be extravagantly dark and glossy.

2 onions, finely chopped
4 skinned, deboned chicken breasts, cut into thin strips
6 carrots, cut into thin matchsticks
1 punnet (about 300 g) button mushrooms, sliced
4 cloves garlic, peeled and crushed
500 ml (2 cups) sugarsnap peas, topped and tailed
30 ml (2 tbsp) cornflour
60 ml (1/4 cup) soft brown sugar
5 ml (1 tsp) salt
60 ml (1/4 cup) brandy or sherry
15 ml (1 tbsp) ground ginger
250 ml (1 cup) dark soy sauce

Dry fry onions and chicken strips (*see page xi*). When onions are golden brown and chicken is cooked through (about 20 seconds), add carrots and mushrooms and cook until the mushroom juices begin to run. Add garlic and sugarsnap peas and cook until peas are bright green but still crisp. In a jug, combine cornflour, sugar, salt, brandy or sherry, ginger and soy sauce. Whisk to a smooth sauce. Pour sauce into chicken mixture and cook over a low heat, stirring constantly, until thickened. Simmer for 2 minutes. Serve with hot jasmine rice and a green salad.

Serves 4

COOK'S TIPS

x The amount of cornflour you will need to thicken the sauce sufficiently will depend on the thickness of the soy sauce and the wateriness of the vegetables. If the sauce seems too runny, add another 5 ml (1 tsp) cornflour, mixed with a little water.

SEXY OPTIONS

Add a tin of drained, sliced bamboo shoots to the sauce.

Mung-bean sprouts add a crunchy, interesting note. Add to the sauce a few minutes before serving so that they are wilted but not too soft.

If you can't find sugarsnap peas, use mange-touts instead.

brazilian chicken

If you don't have much time to cook but have a family of fussy eaters, this recipe is the one for you. This simple-to-prepare dish has turned out to be one of the most popular of all the recipes I have given to my patients over the years.

1 onion, finely chopped
4 skinned, deboned chicken breasts, cut into thin strips
2 bunches spring onions, finely chopped
250 ml (1 cup) hot chutney
125 ml (1/2 cup) water
5 ml (1 tsp) vegetable stock powder
15 ml (1 tbsp) cornflour
500 ml (2 cups) fat-free plain yoghurt
salt and milled black pepper

Dry-fry onion (*see page xi*) until soft and brown. Add chicken strips and spring onions and toss over a high heat until chicken is cooked through but still tender. Add chutney and stir well. In a separate jug, mix water, stock powder and cornflour to a smooth, runny paste. Add to chicken and cook over a low heat, stirring constantly, until thickened. Reduce heat and stir in yoghurt. Season with salt and pepper. Gently warm through for 3 minutes. Serve with rice and sweetcorn.

Serves 4

portuguese chicken burgers

A dish designed for those days when you are overcome by a craving for greasy peri-peri chicken: these 'burgers' have all the flavour, but none of the fat.

4 skinned, deboned chicken breasts

MARINADE
250 ml (1 cup) tomato sauce
2 fresh green chillies, de-seeded and finely chopped
15 ml (1 tbsp) whisky
30 ml (2 tbsp) white wine vinegar
juice of 1 lemon
30 ml (2 tbsp) sugar
3 cloves garlic, peeled and crushed
salt and milled black pepper

TO SERVE
4–8 Portuguese rolls
sliced gherkins
sliced tomatoes
lettuce leaves

Cut chicken breasts in half crossways so you have two equal-sized pieces. Put a chicken breast between two pieces of clingwrap and place on a chopping board. Using a wooden rolling pin or the smooth side of a meat tenderiser, beat each breast until it flattens out to about 0.5 cm thick. To make marinade, combine all ingredients in a jug and mix well. Pour marinade over chicken pieces, cover with clingwrap and refrigerate for at least 3 hours, preferably overnight. Preheat the grill to its hottest setting. Put chicken pieces on a grill pan and place under the grill. Cook, basting frequently and turning once, until chicken is cooked through (about 5 minutes) or braai over medium coals until done. Place each breast on a split Portuguese roll and garnish with gherkins, lettuce and tomatoes.

Serves 4–8

COOK'S TIPS

x *A dollop of fat-free plain yoghurt on top of the chicken will take the heat out of these burgers for those with more delicate palates.*

fettucine with chicken and peppers

A quick-to-make pasta dish with strips of brightly coloured peppers in a delicate sauce.

1 onion, finely chopped
2 cloves garlic, peeled and crushed
2 red peppers, thinly sliced into rings
2 yellow peppers, thinly sliced into rings
125 ml ($^1/_2$ cup) water
4 skinned, deboned chicken breasts, cut into thin strips
45 ml (3 tbsp) cornflour
750 ml (3 cups) fat-free milk
80 ml ($^1/_3$ cup) chopped fresh parsley
45 ml (3 tbsp) sherry
5 ml (1 tsp) salt
2 ml ($^1/_2$ tsp) white pepper
500 g fettucine

Dry-fry onion (*see page xi*). When onion is softened and golden brown, add garlic, red peppers and yellow peppers. Cook, adding water if necessary, until vegetables are softened. Add chicken pieces and dry-fry over a moderate heat until chicken is cooked through but still tender (about 20 seconds). Put cornflour in a teacup and add enough of the milk to mix to a smooth, runny paste. Add paste to chicken along with the rest of the milk. Cook over a low heat, stirring constantly, until sauce is thick. Stir in parsley and sherry. Season with salt and pepper. Reduce heat and simmer for 5 minutes. Meanwhile, cook pasta in plenty of boiling salted water. Drain in a colander, then tip into a deep warmed bowl. Pour over chicken sauce, toss carefully to combine and serve piping hot.

Serves 4

thai green curry

This is another of my favourite dinner-party dishes. Even the fussiest of gourmet guests find it difficult to believe that this fragrant green curry contains no oil and no coconut. Do take the trouble to hunt down the exotic ingredients *(see Cook's tips)* as these make all the difference to the finished dish.

4 skinned, deboned chicken breasts, cut into thin strips
45 ml (3 tbsp) fish sauce
15 ml (1 tbsp) brown sugar
45 ml (3 tbsp) green peppercorns in brine, drained
2 fresh green chillies, de-seeded and finely chopped, or to taste
5 fresh lemon leaves, finely shredded
125 ml ($1/2$ cup) fresh basil leaves, torn into pieces
1 tin (200 g) shrimps in brine, drained
5 ml (1 tsp) coconut essence
1 l (4 cups) fat-free plain yoghurt
salt and milled black pepper

SPICE PASTE
5 ml (1 tsp) coriander seeds
5 ml (1 tsp) cumin seeds
1 stalk fresh lemon grass, sliced (see Cook's tips, page 13)
   or 15 ml (1 tbsp) bottled lemon grass, drained
3–4 fresh green chillies, de-seeded
15 ml (1 tbsp) John West Thai Green Curry Paste (see Cook's tips)
30 ml (2 tbsp) grated fresh ginger
1 bunch spring onions, finely chopped
2 cloves garlic, peeled and crushed

First make the spice paste. Put coriander and cumin seeds into a dry frying pan and roast over a high heat until they begin to crackle (about 1 minute). Grind in a mortar and pestle. Add lemon grass, chillies, green curry paste, ginger, spring onions and garlic and pound to a smooth paste. Reserve. In a clean saucepan, dry-fry chicken pieces *(see page xi)*. When chicken begins to brown, stir in spice paste and cook, stirring constantly, until spices release their aroma (about 1 minute). Add fish sauce, sugar, green peppercorns, chillies and half the lemon leaves and basil. Stir quickly to combine, then add shrimps and coconut essence and simmer for another minute. Reduce heat and stir in yoghurt. Warm through for 3 minutes (no longer, or the yoghurt may curdle). Season with salt and pepper. Sprinkle with remaining lemon and basil leaves and serve immediately with basmati rice.

Serves 4

COOK'S TIPS

x If you don't have fresh ginger, use 15 ml (1 tbsp) bottled ginger paste.

x Fish sauce, bottled lemon grass, ginger paste and green curry paste are now available from all good supermarkets and Oriental delicatessens. I use the John West brand of lemon grass and green curry paste, both of which have an authentic taste.

x Coconut essence may be found at speciality food shops and certain home industries shops and baking outlets. Don't be tempted to use coconut or coconut cream in its place — both are loaded with saturated fat.

x If you don't have a lemon tree in your garden, lemon leaves can be found in Oriental delicatessens.

winter chicken stew

A thick, hearty stew just like the one granny used to make — except this version takes just 10 minutes to whip together before going in the oven. This is a dish designed for a chilly winter's day when a hungry family needs something warm and scrumptious.

1 onion, chopped
4 skinned, deboned chicken breasts, cut into thin strips
250 ml (1 cup) red wine
250 ml (1 cup) water
1 tin (400 g) tomato and onion mix
750 ml (3 cups) frozen baby carrots or diced fresh carrots
4 potatoes, scrubbed and quartered
250 ml (1 cup) frozen peas
15 ml (1 tbsp) dried mixed herbs
250 ml (1 cup) pearl barley
1 tin (400 g) baked beans in tomato sauce
30 ml (2 tbsp) chutney
salt and milled black pepper

Preheat oven to 180 °C. Dry-fry onion (see page xi) until golden brown. Add the chicken strips and toss over a high heat until they turn white. Tip into a deep non-stick ovenproof dish, add all remaining ingredients and mix well to combine. Season with salt and pepper. Cover with foil or a lid and bake for 90 minutes, stirring every 30 minutes and adding more water if necessary. Serve with steamed green vegetables and Spicy Mashed Butternut (see page 27).

Serves 4

COOK'S TIPS

x A sprig of parsley, some finely chopped celery and a bay leaf will add extra flavour to this simple stew. Remove parsley and bay leaf before serving.

x This stew can be cooked on top of the stove. Cover the saucepan, turn the heat down to its lowest setting and simmer for 90 minutes. Stir occasionally to prevent sticking and top up with more water if the stew seems dry.

x If you don't have barley in the cupboard, use 125 ml ($^1/_2$ cup) brown rice instead, but reduce cooking time to 45 minutes.

italian chicken

A really easy family supper dish with a knock-out Italian flavour.

4 skinned, deboned chicken breasts, cut into thin strips
15 ml (1 tbsp) dried oregano
10 ml (2 tsp) dried mixed Italian herbs
1 large brinjal, cubed
2 tins (400 g each) tomato and onion mix
2 cloves garlic, peeled and crushed
salt and milled black pepper

Dry-fry chicken strips and herbs (see page xi). When chicken is golden brown, add all remaining ingredients and mix thoroughly. Reduce heat, cover and simmer very gently for 30 minutes, or until brinjal is cooked through. Serve with rice and Braised Fennel with Tomato (see page 32).

Serves 4

chicken pilaff

This pilaff is quick and easy to make, yet has a surprisingly sophisticated flavour.

1 onion, finely chopped
2 ribs celery, finely sliced
2 green peppers, finely chopped
4 skinned, deboned chicken breasts, cut into thin strips
4 slices shaved smoked ham or turkey, cut into small cubes
500 ml (2 cups) long-grain rice
125 ml ($^1/_2$ cup) dry sherry
10 ml (2 tsp) Worcestershire sauce
500 ml (2 cups) water
1 punnet (about 300 g) button mushrooms, sliced
45 ml (3 tbsp) chopped fresh parsley
salt and milled black pepper
30 ml (2 tbsp) chopped fresh herbs or 15 ml (1 tbsp) dried mixed herbs

Dry-fry onions (see page xi). When onions soften and turn golden brown, add celery and green peppers and dry-fry over a high heat until slightly softened. Add chicken and ham or turkey pieces and dry-fry until chicken begins to brown. Stir in rice and cook until grains begin to toast and turn golden (about 3 minutes). Add sherry, Worcestershire sauce and water. Reduce heat and simmer, covered, for 25 minutes. Stir in mushrooms, parsley and herbs. Simmer for a further 10 minutes, or until mushrooms are cooked through, adding a little more water if necessary. Season with salt and pepper and serve piping hot with Summer Salad (see page 21).

Serves 4–6

COOK'S TIPS

x Chicken Pilaff can be baked in the oven. Dry-fry vegetables, chicken and rice. Tip into a deep non-stick casserole dish. Add remaining ingredients, cover and bake at 180° for about 25 minutes, adding more water if necessary. Stir in mushrooms and herbs, and bake for another 10 minutes.

poached lemon and asparagus chicken

A very stylish and simple dish that will appeal to those with a refined palate.

4 skinned, deboned chicken breasts
375 ml (1$^1/_2$ cups) fat-free milk
5 ml (1 tsp) chicken stock powder
1 small onion, finely chopped
finely grated zest and juice of 1 lemon
15 ml (1 tbsp) fat-free milk powder
80 ml ($^1/_2$ cup) dry white wine
30 ml (2 tbsp) cornflour
45 ml (3 tbsp) water
1 tin (400 g) asparagus cuts, plus their juice
salt and milled black pepper

Cut each chicken breast lengthways into 2 or 3 slices. Heat milk in a saucepan and stir in chicken stock powder and onion. Put in chicken pieces, cover saucepan and poach gently for 10 minutes, or until chicken is cooked but still tender. In a jug, whisk together lemon zest, lemon juice, milk powder, wine and strained liquid from asparagus tin. Add to chicken and stir well. Simmer for a further 10 minutes. Put cornflour in a teacup and add enough water to make a smooth, runny paste. Whisk paste into chicken and cook over a low heat, stirring constantly, until sauce is smooth and thick. Fold in drained asparagus cuts and mix carefully. Simmer for 2 minutes to heat asparagus. Season with salt and pepper. Serve on a bed of rice or with Duchesse Potatoes (see page 30).

Serves 4

lemon chicken and wild rice

An unusual yet surprisingly delicious dish that will delight family and guests alike.

375 ml (1½ cups) brown and wild rice (see Cook's tips)
4 skinned, deboned chicken breasts, cubed
30 ml (2 tbsp) soy sauce
125 ml (½ cup) water
finely grated zest and juice of 1 lemon
45 ml (3 tbsp) chopped fresh parsley
3 cloves garlic, peeled and crushed
salt and milled black pepper

Cook brown and wild rice as directed on the packet. Dry-fry chicken (*see page xi*). When chicken begins to brown, add soy sauce, water and lemon juice and simmer for 1 minute. In a small bowl, combine lemon zest, parsley and garlic. Stir into saucepan and mix carefully, making sure the chicken is well coated. Simmer for another 5 minutes, or until chicken is cooked through. Drain rice and stir into chicken. Mix together carefully and season with salt and pepper. Serve with a green salad.

Serves 4

COOK'S TIPS

x A boil-in-the-bag mix of brown and wild rice is available in major supermarkets. If you can't find it, just use brown rice.

x For a delicious vegetarian version of this dish, omit the chicken and add broccoli, asparagus and baby marrow.

SEXY OPTIONS

Add 10 ml (2 tsp) finely grated fresh ginger and a generous handful of chopped fresh coriander.

roast chicken with bread sauce

Designed for those blue days when a bit of comforting nursery food is in order, this low-fat version of roast chicken and bread sauce will warm your heart as well as your tummy.

45 ml (3 tbsp) cake flour
5 ml (1 tsp) chicken spice
2 ml (½ tsp) salt
2 ml (½ tsp) milled black pepper
4 skinned, deboned chicken breasts

BREAD SAUCE
2 cloves
1 onion, halved
500 ml (2 cups) fat-free milk
1 bay leaf
1 sprig fresh parsley
4 slices brown bread, made into fine breadcrumbs
salt and milled black pepper

Preheat oven to 180 °C. In a shallow dish, combine flour, chicken spice, salt and pepper. Lightly coat each chicken breast in seasoned flour and shake off excess. Place breasts in a plastic cooking bag, seal and place on a baking sheet. Cut a small slit in the bag to allow steam to escape. Bake for 40–45 minutes, or until chicken is cooked through. Meanwhile, make bread sauce. Stick a clove into each onion half. Heat milk in a saucepan and add onion halves, bay leaf and parsley. Just before the milk boils, remove from heat and leave to stand for 15 minutes to allow the flavours to infuse. Remove onions, bay leaf and parsley. Add breadcrumbs and whisk well. Season with salt and pepper and simmer over a low heat for 5 minutes. When chicken is cooked, cut open cooking bag and slide onto a warmed platter. Pour over hot bread sauce. Serve with Roast Potatoes (*see page 29*) and Glazed Baby Carrots (*see page 33*).

Serves 4

CHICKEN

desserts

*O*ur taste buds wouldn't have sweet sensors if we weren't supposed to delight in this taste! A dessert is something to prolong the joy of a delicious meal. It is not meant to stand alone, and it is not meant as a 'filler'. One should eat until full, and then continue the pleasure by finishing off with something sweet, dripping with decadence, that rounds off the symphony of flavours! Without puddings, we are missing out on the 'jewels' of the food world; the part of a meal that sparkles and delights all, but doesn't overpower the main course intended to give us warm substance.

The desserts and puddings in this chapter are close to unbelievable and, what's more, they're a fantastic way to enjoy 'polish' foods such as fruits and dairy products.

baked apples

A homely dessert perfect for cold winter evenings.

4 large apples (red ones are best, but any will do)
125 ml ($^1/_2$ cup) seedless raisins
20 ml (4 tsp) cinnamon
10 ml (2 tsp) nutmeg
250 ml (1 cup) soft brown sugar or 125 ml ($^1/_2$ cup) fructose
   and 125 ml ($^1/_2$ cup) molasses
juice of 1 lemon
1 l (4 cups) hot water
500 ml (2 cups) fat-free plain yoghurt
cinnamon to decorate

Preheat oven to 180 °C. Core the apples and use the tip of a sharp knife to score the skin around the middle of each one. Stand the apples in a deep ovenproof dish. In a separate bowl, mix together the raisins, spices and some of the sugar. Carefully spoon this mixture into the core of each apple, pushing down firmly each time and packing it in tightly. In a jug, mix the remaining sugar with the lemon juice and hot water, and pour into the dish. Cover with foil and bake for 30 minutes. Remove the foil and continue baking for a further 15 minutes, to caramelise the sugar on the apples. Drizzle with chilled yoghurt, sprinkle with cinnamon and serve piping hot.

Serves 4

COOK'S TIPS

x The apples expand in the heat of the oven, so scoring the skin stops them from bursting.

SEXY OPTIONS

Instead of the raisin mixture, use fat-free sweet mincemeat and 30 ml (2 tbsp) rum or brandy to fill the apples.

'bread and butter' pudding

Who would believe a bread and butter pudding could be fat-free? If you've got some stale bread in the kitchen, it's a great excuse to try this traditional family favourite.

8 slices stale white bread
60 ml (4 tbsp) apricot jam
15 ml (1 tbsp) each currants and sultanas, soaked in 30 ml
   (2 tbsp) rum or brandy for 20 minutes
5 egg whites
500 ml (2 cups) fat-free milk
125 ml ($^1/_2$ cup) soft brown sugar
2 ml ($^1/_2$ tsp) cinnamon
2 ml ($^1/_2$ tsp) nutmeg

Preheat oven to 160 °C. Spread the bread with the jam. Trim off the crusts and cut each slice in half diagonally. Layer the bread in a small ovenproof dish, sprinkling currants and sultanas, and any remaining rum or brandy, in between the layers. Beat together the egg whites, milk, sugar and spices, and pour over the bread slices. Leave to stand for 15 minutes then bake, uncovered, for 50 minutes, or until set and golden. Serve hot.

Serves 4

COOK'S TIPS

x Use freshly grated nutmeg if you can as its flavour is much more aromatic. If you store whole nutmegs in an airtight container in a dark cupboard they'll last for months — far longer than the ready-ground variety.

golden sponge pudding with lemon sauce

This sticky steamed sponge is served with a tangy lemon sauce that provides a good contrast with the sweetness of the golden syrup.

SPONGE
80 ml (⅓ cup) apple sauce (see page xiv)
80 ml (⅓ cup) white sugar
2 egg whites
375 ml (1½ cups) self-raising flour, sifted
2 ml (½ tsp) salt
60 ml (¼ cup) fat-free milk

125 ml (½ cup) apple sauce
90 ml (6 tbsp) golden syrup or molasses

SAUCE
125 ml (½ cup) caster sugar
20 ml (4 tsp) cornflour
1 ml (¼ tsp) salt
250 ml (1 cup) water
finely grated zest of 1 lemon
30 ml (2 tbsp) apple sauce
45 ml (3 tbsp) lemon juice

To make the sponge, cream 80 ml (⅓ cup) apple sauce with the sugar until fluffy. Beat in the egg whites and then fold in the sifted flour and salt. Stir in enough milk to make a smooth 'dropping' consistency. Put 125 ml (½ cup) apple sauce into a 1 litre basin. Use a rubber spatula to cover the sides of the basin with golden syrup or molasses. Spoon in the sponge mixture. Cover the basin with foil or greaseproof paper and secure with string. Stand the basin in a large saucepan containing enough boiling water to come halfway up the basin. Cover the pan and steam the pudding for 2½ hours, adding more boiling water to the saucepan as required. Meanwhile, make the lemon sauce. Put the sugar, cornflour and salt into a saucepan and gradually add the water to make a smooth paste. Add any remaining water, the lemon zest and apple sauce and cook over a medium heat, stirring, until sauce is thick and smooth. Add the lemon juice and keep warm. Run a knife around the outside of the pudding and turn it out onto a serving plate. Decorate with a twisted lemon slice and serve with the lemon sauce.

Serves 6–8

rice pudding

Another heart-warming winter dish. In this recipe, the creamy rice is studded with juicy raisins and flavoured with spices.

250 ml (1 cup) long-grain rice
1 l (4 cups) water
2 ml (½ tsp) salt
1 sachet (100 g) fat-free milk powder
250 ml (1 cup) seedless raisins
250 ml (1 cup) soft brown sugar or 125 ml (½ cup) fructose
    and 125 ml (½ cup) molasses
10 ml (2 tsp) cinnamon
5 ml (1 tsp) nutmeg
30 ml (2 tbsp) sherry, optional
4 egg whites
molasses or honey, and cinnamon, to serve

Preheat oven to 180 °C. Put the rice into a saucepan with the water and salt and bring to the boil. Boil for 5 minutes. Stir in the remaining ingredients except the egg whites. Pour the mixture into a deep ovenproof dish and bake for 1 hour. Remove from the oven and allow to cool for 10 minutes. Beat the egg whites until stiff and fold into the rice mixture. Bake for a further 15 minutes. Serve piping hot, drizzled with molasses or honey, and sprinkled with cinnamon.

Serves 4–6

coffee crème brulée

(See overleaf page 87)
My special version of the classic French dish. The crispy caramel topping remains the same, but the creamy custard is flavoured with coffee and, of course, it's fat free.

500 ml (2 cups) fat-free milk
1 sachet (100 g) fat-free milk powder
80 ml ($1/3$ cup) caster sugar
10 ml (2 tsp) instant coffee granules
5 egg whites, beaten
7 ml ($1^1/2$ tsp) vanilla essence
125 ml ($1/2$ cup) soft brown sugar

Preheat oven to 140 °C. Heat the milk, milk powder and caster sugar over a very low heat, stirring constantly. Add the coffee granules and stir until dissolved. Beat the egg whites until smooth and thick, but not stiff. Stir the hot coffee mixture into the egg whites. Add the vanilla essence and stir well, until smooth. Pour the mixture into 4 individual ramekins or other small ovenproof dishes. Put in a roasting tin and pour boiling water into the tin until it almost reaches the tops of the dishes. Bake for 45 minutes. Leave to cool then chill overnight. Just before serving, cover the surface of the puddings with a thick layer of brown sugar, patted down. Preheat the grill to high. Put the dishes into a roasting tin, but this time fill it with iced water until it almost reaches the tops of the dishes. Grill until the sugar has browned and caramelised. Serve immediately, or chill for 2–3 hours.

Serves 4

knickerbocker glory

True to its name, this is a really glorious dessert, with its colourful layers of fruit, jelly, custard and fromage frais.

500 ml (2 cups) fat-free fromage frais
125 ml ($1/2$ cup) caster sugar
2 sachets (80 g each) fruit jelly (one raspberry and one greengage)
500 ml (2 cups) boiling water
500 ml (2 cups) fat-free milk
60 ml (4 tbsp) custard powder
1 tin (about 400 g) peach slices
1 tin (about 400 g) fruit salad
30 ml (2 tbsp) sugar
fresh fruit and fresh lemon balm leaves, to decorate

Beat together the fromage frais and caster sugar. Set aside. Make the jellies with the boiling water as directed on the packet. Set aside. In a large jug, blend 45 ml (3 tbsp) of the milk with the custard powder to form a smooth paste. Bring the remaining milk to the boil. Stir the boiling milk into the custard powder paste. Return to the saucepan and cook over a low heat, stirring until custard thickens. Set aside. Divide the first jelly flavour between 4 tall, slender glasses. Chill until set. Add a layer of fruit, a layer of custard and a layer of fromage frais. Add a layer of the second jelly and repeat the other layers. Garnish with fresh fruit and lemon balm leaves and serve.

Serves 4

COOK'S TIPS

x *To complement the pink and green jellies, use slices of kiwi fruit and strawberries to decorate the desserts.*

baked alaska

(See opposite page xiii)

A spectacular dessert that will prompt gasps of admiration as you bring it to the dining table, and gasps of surprise as you cut into it and reveal the frozen ice-cream in the centre!

fat-free sponge cake (see Cook's tips)
60 ml ($1/4$ cup) sherry
3 ripe bananas
3 large egg whites
80 ml ($1/2$ cup) caster sugar
2 ml ($1/2$ tsp) cream of tartar
1 tub (1 litre) fat-free vanilla ice-cream (see Cook's tips, page 80)
caster sugar for sprinkling

Preheat oven to 220 °C. Put the sponge on a baking tray and sprinkle with the sherry. Peel the bananas and slice in half lengthwise. Whisk the egg whites until stiff then fold in the caster sugar and cream of tartar. Whisk again until very stiff. Put the ice-cream on top of the sponge and trim so that the ice-cream and sponge are the same size and shape. Arrange the banana halves on top of the ice cream then, working swiftly, use a rubber spatula to completely cover the ice-cream and sides of the sponge with the egg whites. Sprinkle with a little caster sugar and place immediately in the oven. Almost immediately, turn off the oven and turn on the grill, so that the peaks of the meringue turn brown. Serve immediately.

Serves 6–8

SEXY OPTIONS

Replace the bananas with halved fresh strawberries and cover the sponge with a layer of strawberry jam before you add the ice-cream.

COOK'S TIPS

x *For the sponge cake, you can use freshly made or left-over Swiss Roll (see page 86), Angel Cake (see page 88) or Golden Sponge Pudding (see page 77).*

x *The whisked egg whites act as an insulator and prevent the ice-cream from melting in the oven. It is important, therefore, to ensure the ice-cream is completely covered with meringue.*

hot port pears with custard

A light dessert that would be perfect after a rich main course. Soaking the pears in port and red wine not only gives them a delicious flavour, it turns them a beautiful ruby colour.

8 ripe pears
20 whole cloves
1 l (4 cups) ruby port
2 cups (500 ml) red wine
250 ml (1 cup) soft brown sugar or fructose
45 ml (3 tbsp) custard powder
1 l (4 cups) fat-free milk
60 ml (4 tbsp) sugar or fructose

Peel the pears, leaving the stalks intact. Push 2 or 3 cloves into each pear. Stand the pears upright in a deep ovenproof dish. Gently heat the port, wine and sugar, stirring until the sugar has dissolved: do not allow to boil. Pour this mixture over the pears, cover and chill overnight. Preheat the oven to 160 °C. Put the dish of pears, uncovered, into the oven and bake for 20–30 minutes, or until the pears are slightly softened. Meanwhile, make the custard as directed on the packet, using the custard powder, fat-free milk and sugar or fructose. Serve the pears piping hot with hot or cold custard.

Serves 4–8

DESSERTS 79

winter pavlova

(See overleaf page 86)
Not all winter desserts have to be steamed puddings! Make the most of the season's berries in this ever-popular dish.

MERINGUE
4 egg whites
250 ml (1 cup) caster sugar
80 ml ($1/2$ cup) granulated white sugar
15 ml (1 tbsp) cornflour

TOPPING
500 ml (2 cups) mixed berries
500 ml (2 cups) fat-free vanilla ice-cream (see Cook's tips)
1 orange, segmented
80 ml ($1/3$ cup) brandy
cocoa powder for sprinkling

Preheat oven to 140 °C. To make the meringue, whisk the egg whites until they are very stiff and form peaks. Gradually add the caster sugar, still whisking, until all of the sugar is combined and the mixture is thick, smooth and glossy. Combine the granulated sugar and cornflour. Gradually fold this into the egg whites, incorporating as much air as possible. Cut a piece of greaseproof paper to fit a baking tray at least 25 cm wide. Spread a third of the meringue mixture onto the paper, to form a circular base about 20 cm in diameter. Smooth out with a rubber spatula. Using a dessertspoon, pile the rest of the mixture around the edge of this circle, to make a hollow nest. Bake for 45 minutes. Leave to cool. Use an ice-cream scoop to fill the centre of the nest with balls of ice-cream, slightly piled up. Sprinkle the berries randomly, using them to fill the crevices between the balls of ice-cream. Arrange the orange segments decoratively on top, drizzle with the brandy and sprinkle cocoa powder over the whole pavlova.

Serves 6

COOK'S TIPS

x Don't worry if the meringue is uneven; this adds to the visual appeal of the dish, so don't try to make it too perfect.

x Woolworth's Slimmer's Choice is a good brand of ice-cream that's fat-free.

granadilla ice-cream

(See opposite)
Everyone loves ice-cream, especially a home-made version that contains no fat!

310 ml ($1 1/4$ cups) granadilla pulp, including pips
250 ml (1 cup) caster sugar
juice of $1/2$ lemon
1 l (4 cups) fat-free plain yoghurt

TOPPING
125 ml ($1/2$ cup) granadilla pulp, including pips
finely grated zest of 1 orange
80 ml ($1/3$ cup) Cointreau

Mix together all ice-cream ingredients until well combined. Turn into a metal container and put into the freezer. Freeze for 1–2 hours, until ice crystals are just beginning to form. Remove from the freezer, beat well and freeze again. Repeat this 3 times, until the ice-cream is thick and smooth. Freeze until completely solid. Mix together the granadilla, orange zest and Cointreau, pour over the ice-cream and serve.

Serves 6–8

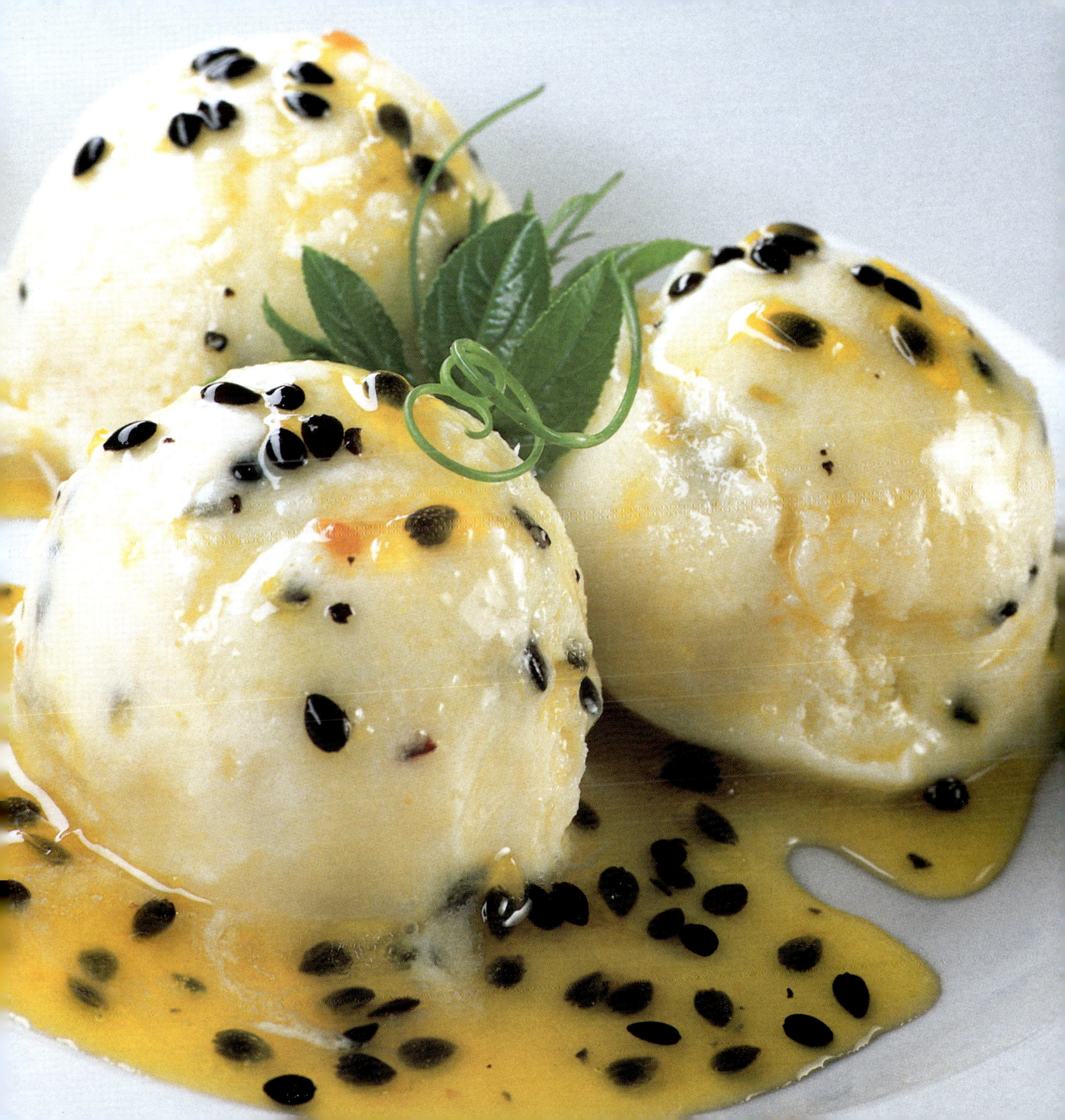

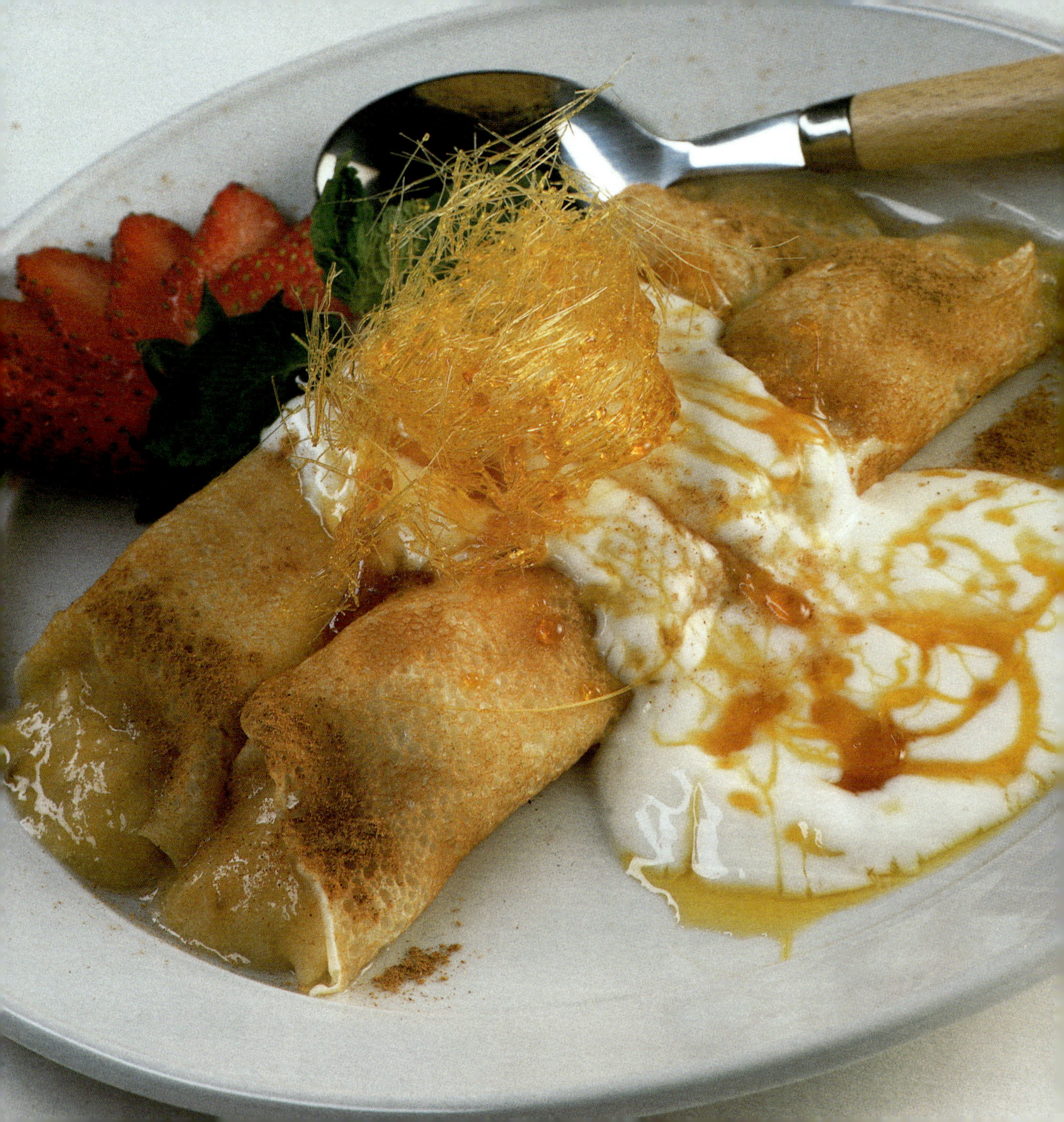

rich banana pancakes

(See opposite)

With a good non-stick frying pan, you can easily cook pancakes without any fat, and with this filling and topping they make a luscious dessert.

PANCAKES
250 ml (1 cup) cake flour
250 ml (1 cup) fat-free milk
125 ml (1/2 cup) sugar
2 egg whites
pinch of salt

FILLING
3 very ripe bananas
15 ml (1 tbsp) caster sugar
10 ml (2 tsp) sherry or kirsch

TOPPINGS
burnt brown sugar (see Cook's tips)
250 ml (1 cup) fat-free plain yoghurt
cinnamon

To make the pancakes, mix together all the ingredients and beat until smooth. Heat a non-stick frying pan and pour in enough of the batter to just cover the base of the pan in a thin layer. Cook for 1–2 minutes per side, until golden. Mash the bananas. Add the caster sugar, vanilla essence and sherry or kirsch and mix until smooth. Spoon the mixture in a strip along the centre of each pancake and roll up. Serve with burnt brown sugar, fat-free yoghurt and a sprinkling of cinnamon.

Makes about 12 pancakes

COOK'S TIPS

x To make burnt brown sugar, put 250 ml (1 cup) brown sugar in a saucepan with 30 ml (2 tbsp) water. Heat over a medium heat, stirring carefully, until the sugar melts and begins to bubble. Continue to heat until sugar is caramelised, dark and smooth. Remove from heat and pour over the pancakes. Be very careful when working with caramelised sugar — it reaches very high temperatures and, because it is so sticky, can cause nasty burns if it splashes onto your skin.

x To keep the pancakes warm while you cook the rest of the batter, pile them on a warmed plate and cover with a tea towel.

strawberry delight

The flavour of summer, served as a pretty pink mousse. This one will be really popular with the kids!

1 l (4 cups) fresh strawberries, washed and hulled
2 sachets (80 g each) strawberry jelly powder
500 ml (2 cups) boiling water
2 sachets (100 g each) fat-free milk powder

TO DECORATE
1 strawberry
2–3 fresh mint leaves
15 ml (1 tbsp) icing sugar

Purée the strawberries in a food processor or blender. Put in the freezer to chill quickly. Meanwhile, dissolve the jelly powder in the boiling water, stirring well. Set aside. When the puréed strawberries are chilled (not frozen), stir in the milk powder. Beat well until light and frothy. Stir this mixture into the warm jelly then pour into a mould. Chill for about 1 hour. Beat the mixture well again then return to the refrigerator. If the fruit pulp sinks to the bottom of the jelly, repeat this procedure again. When set, decorate with a strawberry and a few fresh mint leaves, sift icing sugar over the top and serve.

Serves 4–6

hot and spicy stewed fruit

A warming dessert, bursting with rich and aromatic flavours. Made from store-cupboard ingredients, it's easy to make at any time of the year.

2 apples, cored and cut into chunks
1 pear, cored and cut into chunks
500 ml (2 cups) dried apricots
250 ml (1 cup) seedless raisins
3 lemons, cut into rough chunks
zest of $^1/_2$ orange, cut into thin strips
10 ml (2 tsp) cinnamon
5 ml (1 tsp) ground ginger
5 ml (1 tsp) nutmeg
250 ml (1 cup) soft brown sugar or molasses
500 ml (2 cups) water
125 ml ($^1/_2$ cup) brandy
10 cloves

Preheat oven to 180 °C. Arrange all the fruit in a deep ovenproof dish. Sprinkle over the orange zest. Put the remaining ingredients in a saucepan and heat gently until the sugar has dissolved. Alternatively, heat in the microwave for 3 minutes on high. Pour over the fruit, topping up with water, if necessary, to cover all the fruit. Bake, covered with a lid or foil, for 1 hour, or until the fruit is soft (the lemons will remain hard). Carefully remove the lemon chunks and stir well. Serve piping hot, with chilled fat-free plain yoghurt.

Serves 4–6

COOK'S TIPS

x This dish is also good served chilled. Keep some in the refrigerator and help yourself to a healthy breakfast every morning.

orange sorbet

A sorbet is great served as a refreshing palate-tingler after a rich meal, and this one couldn't be simpler to make.

180 ml ($^3/_4$ cup) caster sugar
250 ml (1 cup) water
1 tin (180 g) concentrated orange juice
1 egg white

Put sugar and water into a saucepan and heat slowly until the sugar has dissolved. Leave to cool. Add the orange juice to the syrup. Beat together well then pour into a shallow, plastic, lidded container. Freeze for 30 minutes or until barely firm. Turn into a bowl and beat until there are no large ice crystals. Whisk the egg white until stiff, then fold into the frozen mixture. Return to the container, cover and freeze until required. Transfer the sorbet to the refrigerator for about 30 minutes before serving, to soften a little.

Serves 3–4

SEXY OPTIONS

You can replace the orange juice with any kind of concentrated fruit juice.

baking

*E*ating well means just that. Eating well, not horribly. So we have devoted an entire chapter to the things that people have always delighted in: cakes, breads and other baked goodies. Nothing is quite like the aroma of baking bread or hot, sweet muffins, and you just can't beat the physical response to a dripping Devil's Chocolate Fudge Brownie or a freshly puffed Angel Food Cake. This chapter just goes to show, the important thing about the X Diet is to ENJOY YOUR FOOD!

orange cheesecake

This tangy delight is best made the night before, to make sure it's properly chilled and set and to let the flavours develop. It's a good party dish, so this recipe makes two cheesecakes — enough for 12 people. Halve the quantities if you only want to make one.

CRUST
80 ml ($^1/_3$ cup) sugar
2 sachets (38 g each) Butter Buds
250 ml (1 cup) hot water
250 ml (1 cup) fresh breadcrumbs
250 ml (1 cup) cornflakes, lightly crushed

FILLING
30 ml (2 tbsp) gelatine
45 ml (3 tbsp) cold water
375 ml (1$^1/_2$ cups) white sugar
250 ml (1 cup) fat-free milk
1 egg yolk, lightly beaten
250 ml (1 cup) Jaffa choice frozen orange, mango or fruit nectar, thawed
60 ml ($^1/_4$ cup) fat-free cream cheese
750 ml (3 cups) fat-free cottage cheese
2 egg whites

To make the crust, dissolve the sugar and Butter Buds in the hot water and stir in the breadcrumbs and cornflakes. Mix well. Lightly coat 2 loose-bottomed 24 cm cake tins with non-stick spray. Divide crust mixture between cake tins and press into the bottom. Chill until set. To make the filling, mix gelatine with the cold water and leave to stand. Put sugar, milk and egg yolk in a large bowl and mix well. Heat in the microwave for 6–8 minutes on high, stirring 3 or 4 times, until sugar dissolves and mixture thickens slightly. Add gelatine mixture and stir until it dissolves. Add orange concentrate and stir well to combine. Beat together cream cheese and cottage cheese until smooth, then add to orange mixture. Beat egg whites until stiff. Fold into orange mixture. Pour mixture into the prepared tins. Chill for about 2 hours, until set. Run a sharp knife or spatula around the edge of the tin then carefully release the spring. Decorate with fresh or tinned fruit of your choice and serve.

Each cheesecake serves 6

yoghurt crunchies

Make your own muesli bars with this simple recipe — shop-bought ones are usually laden with nuts, coconut and other hidden fats and are a far cry from the health foods they claim to be!

CRUNCHIES
250 ml (1 cup) nutty wheat flour
625 ml (2$^1/_2$ cups) oats
250 ml (1 cup) soft brown sugar
5 ml (1 tsp) bicarbonate of soda
5 ml (1 tsp) salt
250 ml (1 cup) glacé cherries, halved
250 ml (1 cup) dried dates, chopped
500 ml (2 cups) buttermilk

ICING
125 ml ($^1/_2$ cup) fat-free plain yoghurt
juice of 3 lemons
500 ml (2 cups) icing sugar
5 ml (1 tsp) vanilla essence

Preheat oven to 140 °C. Mix together all ingredients for crunchies and pour into a non-stick baking tin (35 x 25 cm). Press the mixture into the corners and smooth the top. Bake for 30 minutes. Reduce the oven temperature to 100 °C. Cut the mixture, still in the tin, into 5 cm squares. Return to the oven for a further 30 minutes. Leave to cool thoroughly. Meanwhile, make the icing. Combine all the ingredients and beat until smooth. Use a rubber spatula to smooth the icing over the cold crunchies, and put the tray in the refrigerator for 1–2 hours, until the icing has set. Remove the crunchies from the tray and serve.

Makes 35 squares

lena's quick muffins

This recipe is a legend — in no uncertain terms. It was made by mistake, when we tried to make a fruity bread and Lena, our invaluable culinary master, turned the mixture into muffins. Ever since, my colleagues and patients alike have taken to them like bees to honey, and a bowl of muffins never lasts for more than 2 hours in our practice! They are unbelievably quick, easy, and delicious.

875 ml (3½ cups) nutty wheat flour or 500 ml (2 cups) nutty wheat flour and 375 ml (1½ cups) oat bran
500 ml (2 cups) buttermilk or fat-free plain yoghurt
5 ml (1 tsp) salt
5 ml (1 tsp) bicarbonate of soda
250 ml (1 cup) soft brown sugar or fructose
250–500 ml (1–2 cups) fruit (see Sexy options)

Preheat oven to 180 °C. Put all the ingredients in a bowl and mix well. Spoon into non-stick muffin pans and bake for 15 minutes (or until a knife inserted into the centre of a muffin comes out clean). Serve immediately, with fat free cottage cheese and your favourite jam.

Makes about 16

COOK'S TIPS

x If they're not all eaten at once, the muffins will keep for about 3 days in an airtight container. They can be reheated in the microwave for 2–4 seconds on high.

SEXY OPTIONS

Add any of the following fruits to the basic recipe: raisins, sultanas, chopped dates, chopped prunes, mashed banana, cubed tinned pineapple, chopped tinned apples plus a handful of raisins and 10 ml (2 tsp) cinnamon, tinned blueberries, or dried apricots, pears or peaches, rehydrated with hot sugar water.

fluffy yoghurt and banana flan

This is a scrumptious flan with a crispy base and light, creamy filling. It can be prepared well in advance, so it's great for entertaining.

CRUST
500 ml (2 cups) cornflakes, finely crushed
375 ml (1½ cups) oat bran
80 ml (⅓ cup) apple sauce (see page xiv)
juice of 2 lemons
80 ml (⅓ cup) molasses

FILLING
30 ml (2 tbsp) water
10 ml (2 tsp) gelatine
5 ripe bananas
30 ml (2 tbsp) lemon juice
180 ml (¾ cup) fat free plain yoghurt
10 ml (2 tsp) sugar
125 ml (½ cup) fat-free milk
2 egg whites

To make the crust, mix the cornflakes with the oat bran. Put the apple sauce, lemon juice and molasses in a saucepan and heat until runny. Pour into the cornflake mixture and mix well to combine. Turn the mixture into a 30 cm flan dish and press it evenly over the bottom and up the sides. Leave to cool. To make the filling, mix the water and gelatine and set aside. Mash the bananas with the lemon juice, yoghurt and sugar. Whisk the egg whites until thick, and then fold in the banana mixture and gelatine. Spoon into the flan case, smooth the top and chill for 3–4 hours, until set.

Serves 4–6

swiss roll

The perfect Swiss roll must be light and fluffy so be sure to incorporate as much air into the mixture as possible. Unless you've got the muscles of a prize fighter, use an electric whisk.

10 egg whites
180 ml ($3/4$ cup) caster sugar or fructose
180 ml ($3/4$ cup) cake flour
2 ml ($1/2$ tsp) salt
5 ml (1 tsp) baking powder
5 ml (1 tsp) vanilla essence
30 ml (2 tbsp) boiling water
caster sugar or fructose for sprinkling
125 ml ($1/2$ cup) smooth apricot jam
60 ml ($1/4$ cup) fat-free cottage cheese

Preheat oven to 200 °C. Whisk the egg whites until thick but not stiff. Add the sugar or fructose, while whisking, and continue whisking until it is all incorporated. Sift together the flour, salt and baking powder and fold into the egg whites, incorporating as much air as possible. Stir in the vanilla essence and the boiling water. Line a Swiss-roll tin or flat baking tray (35 x 25 cm) with greaseproof paper and sprinkle a generous layer of caster sugar or fructose over the paper. Gently pour the mixture into the lined tray, and bake for 15–20 minutes until golden. Meanwhile, lay a clean, damp tea towel on your work surface. Generously sprinkle the tea towel with more sugar or fructose, and carefully turn the cake out on top. Use a sharp knife to trim away the edges of the cake then roll up the sponge and the damp tea towel. When cool, gently unroll, remove the tea towel and spread the cake with apricot jam and fat-free cottage cheese. Roll up again (without the tea towel!). Slice and serve as fresh as possible.

Serves 8

SEXY OPTIONS

Make the sponge as above, but replace the jam with chocolate fudge icing (see *page 87*). Use only a small amount of icing as it will dribble out and also make the cake soggy. Spread the fat-free cottage cheese first then the fudge icing on top.

sultana tea bread

(See opposite)
Soaking the sultanas overnight in tea makes them plump and juicy and gives a lovely moist loaf.

500 ml (2 cups) sultanas
250 ml (1 cup) cold black tea
250 ml (1 cup) fat-free milk
1 large egg, lightly beaten
500 ml (2 cups) cake flour
37 ml ($2^{1}/2$ tbsp) baking powder
250 ml (1 cup) brown sugar

Soak the sultanas overnight in the cold tea. Preheat oven to 180°C. Mix together the soaked sultanas and tea, milk, egg, flour, baking powder and sugar until smooth. Spray a non-stick loaf tin (20 x 10 x 7 cm) with non-stick spray and line the bottom with greaseproof paper. Pour the mixture into the tin and smooth the top. Bake for 15 minutes then reduce the oven temperature to 150 °C and cook for a further $1^{1}/4$ hours. Leave to cool slightly in tin then remove from tin and cool completely.

Makes about 12 slices

SEXY OPTIONS

Give the loaf a sweet, sticky topping by glazing it with honey. Warm the honey first (see *page 23*) then brush over the top of the loaf.

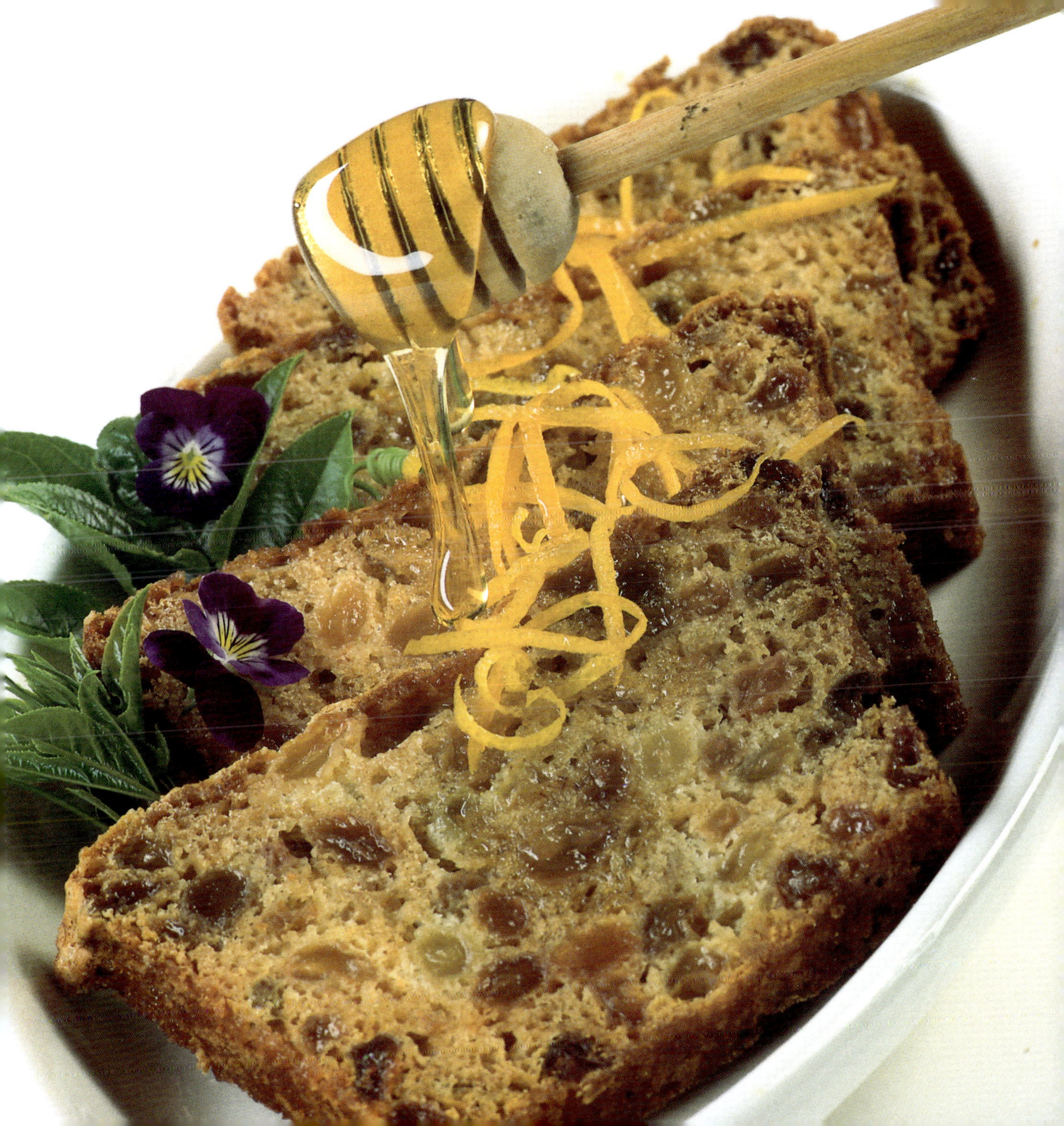

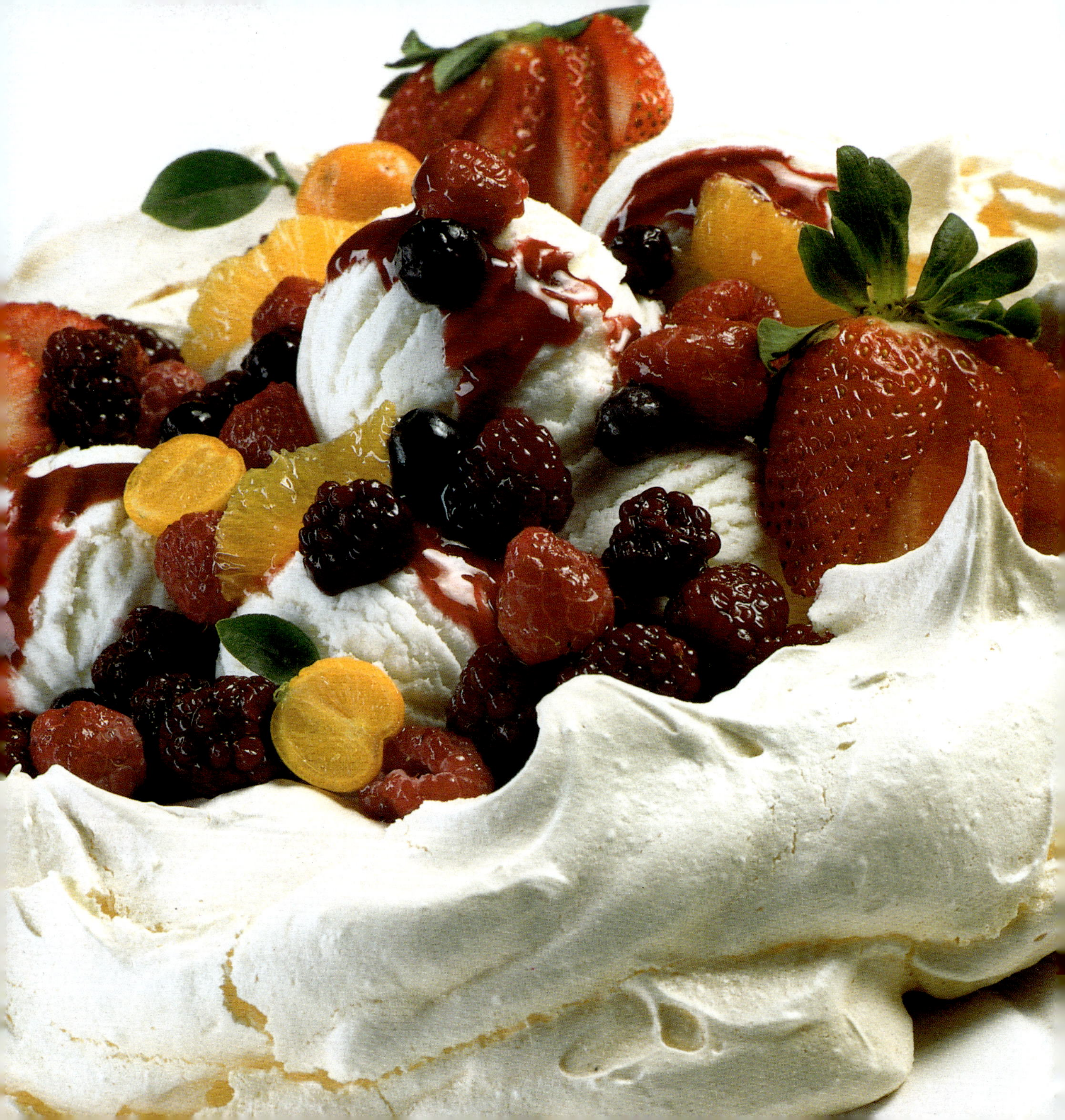

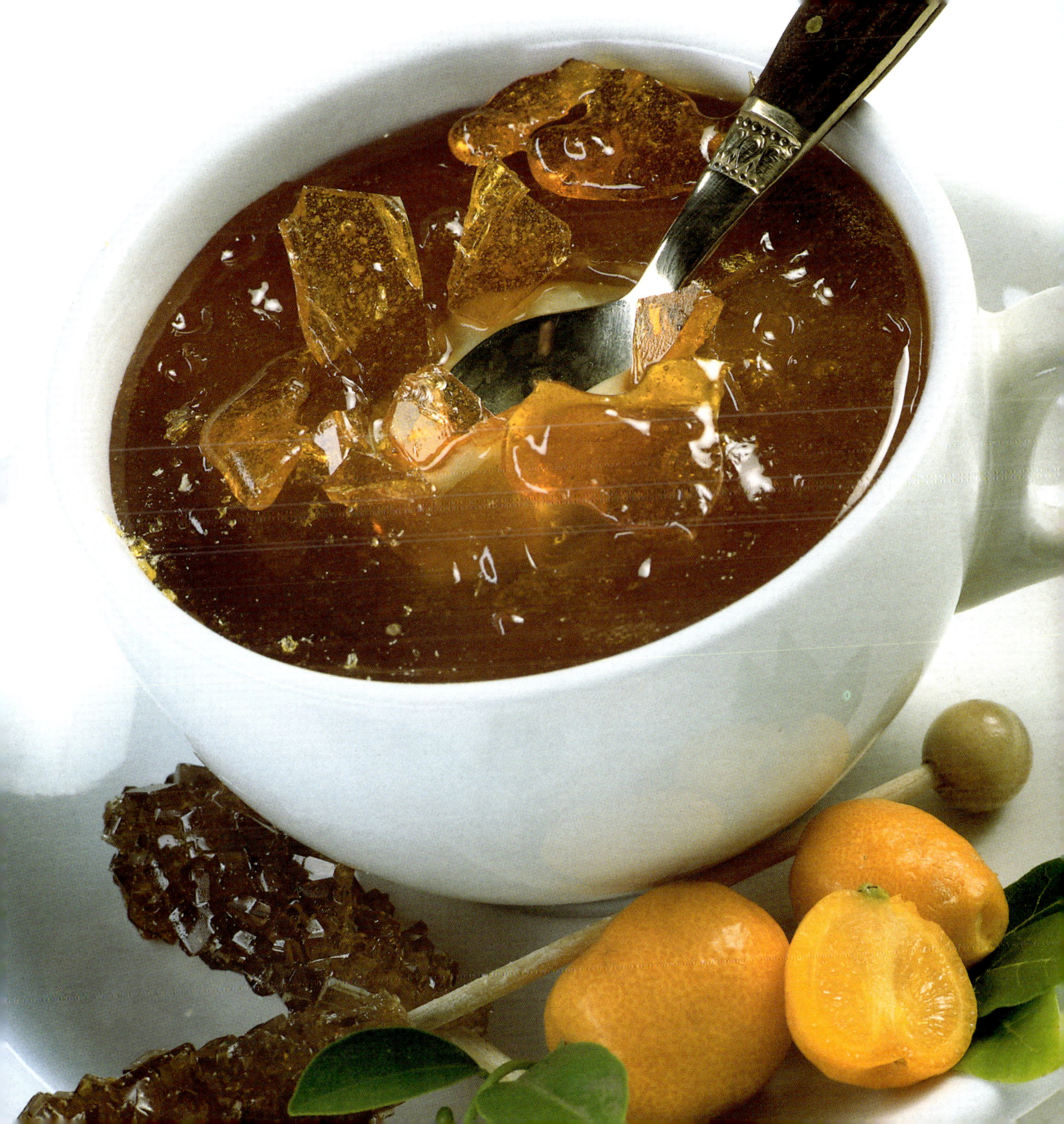

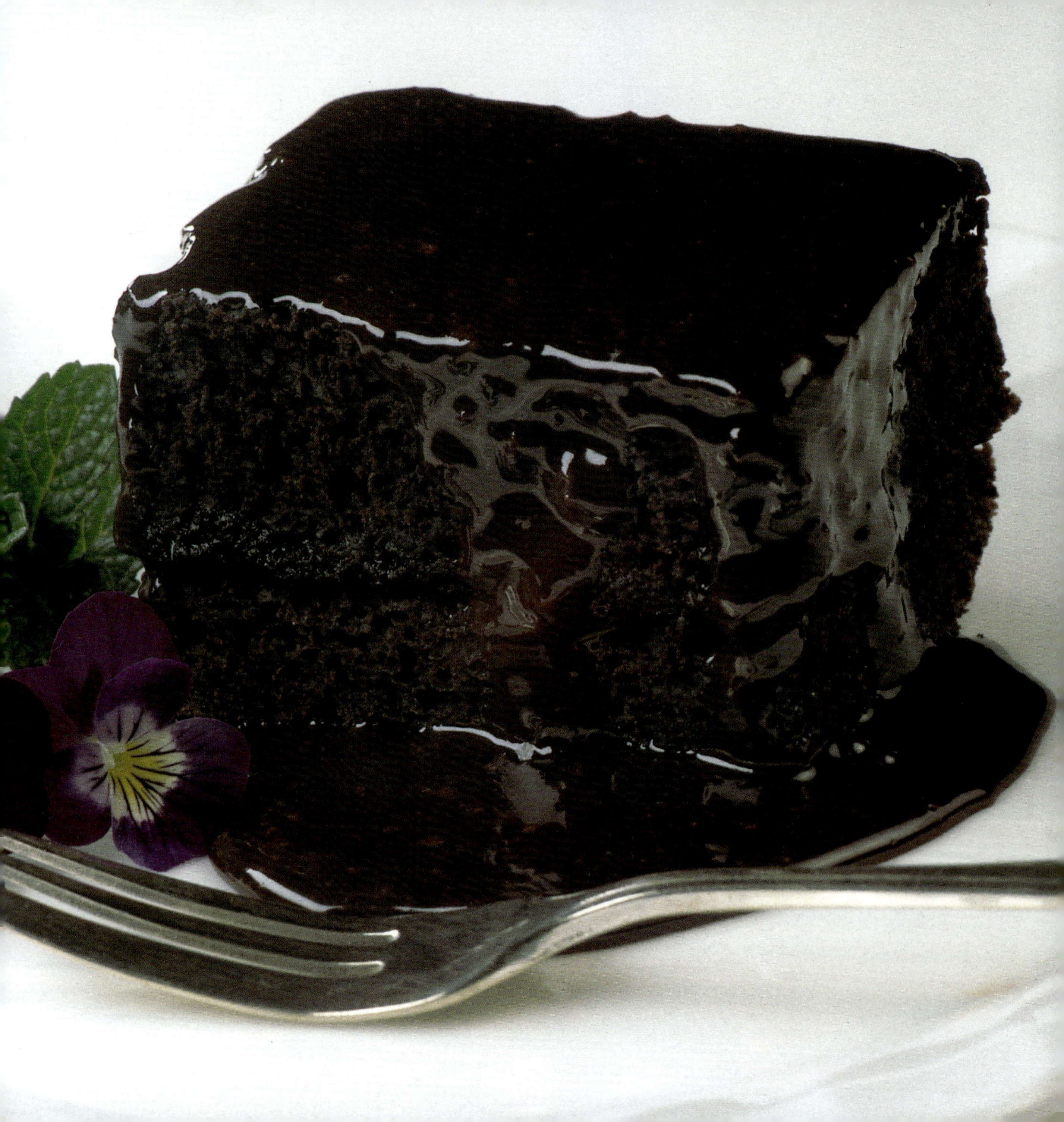

devil's chocolate fudge brownies

(See opposite)
For chocoholics everywhere! No one will believe that this scrumptious, sticky concoction, dripping with fudge icing, is actually fat-free! The fudge icing can also be used as a topping for fat-free ice cream or as a filling for cakes.

BROWNIES
375 ml (1½ cups) cake flour
250 ml (1 cup) white sugar
45 ml (3 tbsp) cocoa powder
6 ml (1 rounded tsp) baking powder
5 ml (1 tsp) bicarbonate of soda
pinch of salt
10 ml (2 tsp) vanilla essence
15 ml (1 tbsp) vinegar
125 ml (½ cup) apple sauce (see page xiv)
250 ml (1 cup) tepid water

FUDGE ICING
125 ml (½ cup) fat-free milk
10 ml (2 tsp) vanilla essence
250 ml (1 cup) apple sauce
250 ml (1 cup) icing sugar
250 ml (1 cup) white sugar
250 ml (1 cup) cocoa powder

Preheat oven to 200 °C. To make the brownies, sift the dry ingredients into a deep non-stick baking tin or roasting tin, about 27 x 18 cm. Mix very well until evenly combined and then level the surface. Make 3 wells in this dry mixture. Mix together vanilla essence, vinegar and apple sauce and pour into the wells. Pour over the water. Mix very well — including all the corners — until the mixture is very smooth. Bake for 15 minutes, then reduce the oven temperature to 150 °C and bake for a further 5 minutes. Meanwhile, make the fudge icing. Combine all the ingredients in a saucepan and heat, stirring, until well combined. Allow the cake to cool slightly in the tin before pouring over the fudge icing. Cut into squares and serve immediately.

Makes 10–12 squares

christmas mince pies

1 egg white, lightly beaten
60 ml (4 tbsp) fat-free milk
½ roll (250 g) phyllo pastry (see Cook's tips, page 3)
500 ml (2 cups) fruit mincemeat
80 ml (⅓ cup) medium cream or sweet sherry
caster sugar for sprinkling

Preheat oven to 180 °C. Mix together the egg white and milk. Cut the phyllo pastry into 40 strips 5 x 30 cm and brush each strip with the egg and milk mixture. Put about 1 tablespoon of the mincemeat at the bottom of a strip, and fold over the bottom of the pastry to form a square. Fold this over again, and continue until you get to the end of the strip. Place the square, with the open sides horizontal, at the base of another pastry strip. Fold in the same manner, to make a neat package. Brush the top with sherry, sprinkle with caster sugar and place on a baking tray. Repeat until the mincemeat is used up. Bake the pies for about 15 minutes, until the pastry is browned at the edges. Leave to cool slightly, until just comfortable to hold. Serve as they are or as a pudding, piping hot with fat-free ice-cream (see Cook's tips, page 80).

Makes about 20

COOK'S TIPS

x Be sure not to use mincemeat made with suet. Look for a fat-free brand.

angel cake

This heavenly cake is lightly flavoured with almonds or vanilla. It can be served with icing or jam but is just as good simply decorated with a dusting of icing sugar.

250 ml (1 cup) cake flour
310 ml (1¼ cups) caster sugar
10 egg whites
5 ml (1 tsp) cream of tartar
2 ml (½ tsp) salt
1 ml (¼ tsp) almond essence or 2 ml (½ tsp) vanilla essence
icing sugar, fat-free icing (see Sexy options) or jam, to serve

Preheat oven to 160 °C. Sift together the flour and half of the sugar several times to incorporate as much air as possible. In a separate bowl, whisk the egg whites until foamy, then add cream of tartar and salt and continue to whisk until the whites are stiff but not dry. Add 30 ml (2 tbsp) of the remaining sugar to the whites and whisk. Continue adding the sugar, 30 ml (2 tbsp) at a time and whisking well after each addition, until all the sugar is incorporated. Sift the flour and sugar mixture in thin layers over the egg whites and fold in each layer carefully. Fold in the almond or vanilla essence. Spoon the mixture carefully into a non-stick 24 cm cake tin. Lightly tap the tin on a flat surface, to remove any large air bubbles. Bake for 1 hour without opening the oven. Leave the cake in the tin but turn it upside down onto a cooling rack. Leave to cool for about 1 hour. Run a sharp knife around the sides of the tin to loosen the cake, and carefully remove from the tin. Dust the top with sifted icing sugar or spread with fat-free icing or jam.

Serves 6–8

SEXY OPTIONS

Make a fat-free icing by mixing together 30 ml (2 tbsp) fat-free milk, 250 ml (1 cup) icing sugar and 60 ml (¼ cup) fat-free cream cheese.

Replace the vanilla or almond essence with 15 ml (1 tbsp) finely grated lemon or orange zest. If you're using icing you can also add some zest to that.

buttermilk rusks

I just had to include a fat-free recipe for this South African favourite. They're so simple to make and keep well in an airtight container.

375 ml (1½ cups) cake flour
10 ml (2 tsp) baking powder
2 ml (½ tsp) bicarbonate of soda
5 ml (1 tsp) salt
375 ml (1½ cups) wholewheat or nutty wheat flour
250 ml (1 cup) seedless raisins
2 egg whites, lightly beaten
180 ml (¾ cup) brown sugar
375 ml (1½ cups) buttermilk
30 ml (2 tbsp) apple sauce (see page xiv)

Preheat oven to 180 °C. Sift cake flour into a bowl. Add baking powder, bicarbonate of soda and salt and sift again. Add wholewheat or nutty wheat flour and raisins. Mix together the egg whites, sugar, buttermilk and apple sauce until well combined. Add to flour mixture and stir just enough to blend together. Do not beat. Turn into a non-stick baking tray (35 x 25 cm) and bake for about 1 hour, until golden. Reduce oven temperature to 80 °C. Remove rusks from oven and cut to your preferred shape and size. Return to oven and leave overnight, or for at least 4–5 hours. Leave to cool completely before storing in an airtight container.

Makes 20–30

sauces

Sauces give a richness to foods that might otherwise be rather bland and dry. It's important to keep your taste buds tingling while on the X Diet, so you must never deprive yourself of your saucy favourites. Here is a selection of fat-free recipes that will bring out the best in most meals. And don't forget the sauces that appear alongside other recipes throughout this book — there's nothing to stop you using them with other dishes. To help you find them, all the sauces in the book are listed separately in the index.

basic gravy

1 onion, finely sliced into rings
500 ml (2 cups) hot water
30 ml (2 tbsp) sherry
5 ml (1 tsp) chicken stock powder
45 ml (3 tbsp) Bisto gravy powder
10 ml (2 tsp) dried mixed herbs
5 ml (1 tsp) finely chopped fresh rosemary
5 ml (1 tsp) finely chopped fresh thyme
15 ml (1 tbsp) orange marmalade
salt and milled black pepper

Dry-fry onion (see page xi). Combine water, sherry, stock powder and Bisto to make a smooth, runny paste. Add to saucepan with herbs and marmalade. Cook, stirring constantly, until gravy thickens. Season generously with salt and pepper.

tomato and onion gravy

1 onion, finely chopped
2 tomatoes, peeled and chopped
30 ml (2 tbsp) Bisto gravy powder
250 ml (1 cup) water
125 ml ($^1/_2$ cup) white wine
salt and milled black pepper

Dry-fry onion (see page xi). When onion is soft and golden, add tomatoes. Cover saucepan and simmer very gently for 10 minutes, or until tomato pieces have collapsed. Mix Bisto with enough water to make a smooth, runny paste. Add to saucepan along with remaining water and wine. Cook, stirring constantly, until gravy thickens to a glossy dark brown. Season with salt and pepper and serve hot.

tuna sauce

1 onion, finely chopped
1 green pepper, finely chopped
250 ml (1 cup) basic white sauce 1 (see page 91)
45 ml (3 tbsp) white wine
1 tin (200 g) tuna in brine, drained and flaked
45 ml (3 tbsp) tomato sauce
30 ml (2 tbsp) chopped capers
juice of $^1/_2$ lemon
5 ml (1 tsp) cayenne pepper, or to taste
salt and milled black pepper

Dry-fry onion and green pepper (see page xi). Stir in white sauce, wine, tuna, tomato sauce, lemon juice and cayenne pepper and heat through. Season with salt and pepper and serve hot over rice, baked potatoes or pasta.

mexican sauce

1 green pepper, finely chopped
1 clove garlic, peeled and crushed
1 large ripe tomato, peeled and chopped
250 ml (1 cup) basic white sauce 1 (see page 91)
1 tin (400 g) baked beans in tomato sauce
5–10 ml (1–2 tsp) Tabasco sauce, to taste
1 small tub (175 ml) fat-free plain yoghurt
salt and milled black pepper

Dry-fry green pepper and garlic (see page xi). Add tomato and cook until tomato softens. Stir in white sauce, baked beans and Tabasco sauce and heat through. Season with salt and pepper and serve hot on toast, fat-free tortillas or baked potatoes, with yoghurt drizzled over the top.

basic white sauce 1

500 ml (2 cups) fat-free milk
37 ml (2½ tbsp) cornflour
10 ml (2 tsp) stock powder
10 ml (2 tsp) salt
5 ml (1 tsp) milled black pepper

Heat 375 ml (1½ cups) of the milk in a saucepan. Combine remaining milk, cornflour, stock powder and salt and mix to a smooth, runny paste. When milk is very hot but not boiling, remove from heat and add cornflour paste, stirring very briskly. Return saucepan to the heat and cook, stirring continuously, until sauce is thick and creamy. Season with pepper.

basic white sauce 2

This version is closer to the classic Béchamel sauce, and is useful when you need a more opaque and creamy-looking sauce.

625 ml (2½ cups) fat-free milk
45 ml (3 tbsp) cake flour
125 ml (½ cup) warm water
5 ml (1 tsp) stock powder
salt and milled black pepper

Heat milk in a saucepan. Combine flour with 15 ml (1 tbsp) warm water and stock powder and mix to a thick paste. Add a little more water and mix again. Continue until you have a very smooth, runny paste. When the milk is very hot but not boiling, remove from heat and whisk in the flour paste, using a wire whisk. Return to the heat and cook, stirring continuously, until sauce is thick and creamy. Simmer for a few minutes to cook out any floury taste. Season with salt and pepper.

COOK'S TIPS

x *If you're not going to use the sauce immediately, lay a piece of clingwrap on the surface to prevent a skin forming.*

x *Any of the following flavourings, or a combination, can be added to the sauce after it has been cooked: 5–10 ml (1–2 tsp) prepared English mustard or Dijon mustard; 125 ml (½ cup) finely chopped fresh parsley, chives, tarragon or chervil; the juice of 1 lemon; freshly grated nutmeg; finely grated onion; finely chopped spring onions; 15–30 ml (1–2 tbsp) Worcestershire sauce; 15–30 ml (1–2 tbsp) soy sauce; 5 ml (1 tsp) anchovy essence; 5–10 ml (1–2 tsp) mild curry powder; 5–10 ml (1–2 tsp) cayenne pepper or chilli powder.*

honey and mustard dressing

This is my favourite fat-free dressing. Make a big jar of it and take it with you when you go out to dinner.

80 ml (⅓ cup) balsamic vinegar
80 ml (⅓ cup) wholegrain French mustard
80 ml (⅓ cup) runny honey
salt and milled black pepper

Combine all ingredients in a screw-top jar and shake well to combine. Store in the refrigerator.

tartare sauce

125 ml (½ cup) fat-free smooth cottage cheese
125 ml (½ cup) fat-free plain yoghurt
½ onion, finely chopped
15 ml (1 tbsp) chopped gherkins
15 ml (1 tbsp) chopped capers
15 ml (1 tbsp) chopped fresh parsley
15 ml (1 tbsp) chopped fresh dill
10 ml (2 tsp) freshly squeezed lemon juice
salt and milled black pepper

Combine all ingredients and mix well. Cover and store in the refrigerator.

SAUCES AND DRESSINGS

recipe index

Angel Cake 88
Apple, Celery and Chickpea Salad 19
Artichoke and Mushroom Fettucine 36
Asparagus and Artichoke Soup 9
Asparagus with Tangy Sauce 2
Baby Marrows Provençal 34
Baked Alaska 79
Baked Apples 76
Bangers and Mash 46
Basic Gravy 90
Basic Vegetable Soup 10
Basic White Sauce 1 91
Basic White Sauce 2 91
Beetroot Soup 15
Bobotie 45
Boerewors with Tomato and Chilli Salsa 6
Braised Fennel with Tomato 32
Brazilian Chicken 69
'Bread and Butter' Pudding 76
Bread Sauce 74
Broccoli Gratin 32
Brown Onion Soup 12
Burnt Sherry and Mushroom Soup 14
Buttermilk Rusks 88
Butternut on the Braai 27
Carefree Paella 60
Carrot and Orange Salad 20
Carrots in Yoghurt 29
'Cheesy' Stuffed Potatoes 31
Chicken à la King 66
Chicken and Pineapple Kebabs 68
Chicken Pilaff 73
Chicken Schnitzels 45
Chicken Stew 46
Chilli Chicken 68
Chinese Chicken 69
Christmas Mince Pies 87
Clam Chowder 8
Coffee Crème Brûlée 78
Couscous Salad 22
Creamed Spinach 26
Creamy Chicken and Brinjal Curry 65
Creamy Herb Kingklip 56
Creamy Mushroom Pasta 35
Crispy 'Fried' Fish 43
Crispy Potato Croquettes 30
Curried Brinjals with Greek Rice 35
Curried Chickpeas 28
Curried Crayfish 59
Curried Mushroom Soup 15
Curried Parsnip and Apple Soup 8
Curried Rice and Peach Salad 19

Curried Three-Bean Salad 24
Devil's Chocolate Fudge Brownies 87
Devilled Crab 54
Double-quick Tomato Pasta 38
Farfalle with Pumpkin Sauce 38
Fat-free Lasagne 42
Fettucine with Chicken and Peppers 70
Fish Cakes 40
Fish in Piquant Tomato Sauce 55
Fluffy Yoghurt and Banana Flan 85
Foil-wrapped Spaghetti with Shellfish 60
Fruity Butternut Soup 11
Garlic Bread 5
Glazed Baby Carrots 33
Golden Chicken Nuggets 67
Golden Potato Wedges 30
Golden Sponge Pudding with Lemon Sauce 77
Granadilla Ice-cream 80
Greek-style Butternut 33
Greek-style Hake 54
Grilled Fish with Spiced Yoghurt 59
Grilled Mushrooms 33
Haddock Paella 54
Honey and Mustard Dressing 91
Hot and Spicy Stewed Fruit 82
Hot Port Pears with Custard 79
Hummus with Pita Wedges 6
Italian Chicken 72
Kingklip Magic 61
Kingklip with Mediterranean Salsa 61
Knickerbocker Glory 78
Lemon Chicken and Wild Rice 74
Lemon Garlic Green Beans 34
Lemon Sauce 77
Lena's Quick Muffins 85
Luxury Oven-poached Sole 57
Macaroni 'Cheese' 48
Marinated Tomatoes 22
Mediterranean Garlic Mussels 4
Mediterranean Salsa 61
Mexican Chilli 43
Mexican Corn Soup 10
Mexican Pasta Casserole 47
Mexican Sauce 90
Millionaire's Fish Pie 51
Minestrone 16
Mushroom and Tuna Bake 53
No-Guilt Hamburgers 41
Orange Cheesecake 84
Orange Foil-baked Haddock 55
Orange Sorbet 82
Ostrich Steak and 'Sour Cream' Potatoes 44
Oven-Baked Crisps 29
Parsnip Purée 28
Pasta Marinara 50

Penne with Spinach and Yoghurt Sauce 37
Poached Lemon and Asparagus Chicken 73
Poached Sole 51
Portuguese Chicken Burgers 70
Potato and Mushroom Bake 31
Potato Salad 18
Prawn and Cucumber Mousse 2
Prawn Pilaff 50
Prawn Risotto 58
Prawn Salad with Hot Orange Dressing 24
Prawn Spring Rolls 5
Prawns Madagascar 57
Quick Chicken Curry 64
Red Cabbage with Apple 34
Red Coleslaw 20
Rice Pudding 77
Rice, Pineapple and Sprout Salad 23
Rich Banana Pancakes 81
Roast Chicken with Bread Sauce 74
Roast Potatoes 29
Roast Vegetable Pasta 37
Roasted Garlic with Bagel Melbas 3
Smoked Chicken and Mushroom Tagliolini 67
Sole with Spinach and Scallop Sauce 62
Sole with Three-mustard and Dill Sauce 52
Sopa di Fideos 36
Spaghetti Bolognese 44
Spiced Yoghurt Chicken 64
Spicy Bean Samoosas 3
Spicy Mashed Butternut 27
Strawberry Delight 81
Sultana Tea Bread 86
Summer Salad 21
Swiss Roll 86
Tartare Sauce 91
Thai Chicken Kebabs 66
Thai Green Curry 71
Thai Hot Prawn Soup 13
Three-pepper and Tuna Bake 58
Tomato and Chilli Salsa 6
Tomato and Onion Gravy 90
Tuna Pasta Salad 23
Tuna Sauce 90
Tzatziki 4
Vegetable Curry 47
Vegetable Lasagne 41
Very Simple Haddock 53
Vichyssoise 14
White Gazpacho 9
Wholesome Chicken Soup 12
Wine-baked Asparagus Kingklip 52
Winter Chicken Stew 72
Winter Pavlova 80
X Diet Pizza 40
Yoghurt Crunchies 84